FROM YOUR ICE CREAM MAKER

ice creams – frozen yogurts – sorbets – sherbets – shakes – sodas

Coleen and Bob Simmons

BRISTOL PUBLISHING ENTERPRISES
San Leandro, California

A Nitty Gritty® Cookbook

Printed in the United States of America.

ISBN 1-55867-105-6

Cover design: Frank Paredes
Cover photography: John Benson
Food stylist: Suzanne Carreiro
Illustrator: James Balkovek

CONTENTS

MAKING ICE CREAM: TIPS AND TECHNIQUES

Everybody LOVES ice cream! Most people have fond childhood memories of ice cream. For some, it might be a birthday party or a visit to an ice cream parlor for a special occasion. We remember hand-cranked ice cream on Nebraska farms. There were ice cream socials put on by local churches as fund-raising events. On the farm, cream and eggs were abundant, and no one was watching his diet. The ladies would vie to see who could produce the richest ice cream. During the fall of late Depression days, just before the start of the Second World War, Bob remembers his family waiting for the horse watering tank to freeze over so his father could take an ax and chop out enough ice to make homemade ice cream.

Now we make ice cream not only because we love the dense, creamy texture, but also because we can be certain of exactly what is in it. Inexpensive commercial ice creams tend to have questionable ingredients added, simply for the purpose of reducing cost or increasing volume. The ice cream you make at home has only milk, eggs, sugar and flavoring. It is much more satisfying than the overly sweet fluff that is sold in ½-gallon blocks. Besides, waiting for the ice cream to freeze is much more romantic than just opening a carton, and the anticipation only adds to the enjoyment of opening the ice cream freezer and serving the ice cream.

We include a broad range of frozen dessert recipes and have tried to make each recipe complete, so you don't have to flip pages to follow it. The one exception is the procedure for drained yogurt, which is described in this section, but once you have made it, it will be very easy to do again without looking at the instructions. Most recipes are designed to yield about 1 quart of ice cream. The yield will vary depending on the freezer used and the speed of freezing. All mixes expand as they freeze, so a good rule is not to fill a freezer container more than ¾ full.

TYPES OF FROZEN DESSERTS

- **Ice cream** is dense, rich and creamy. It usually contains cream and eggs or egg yolks.
- **Gelato** (which is the Italian word for ice cream) contains less air and is a thick, substantial ice cream with more eggs and egg yolks.
- **Sherbet** is less rich than ice cream. It is made with light cream or milk, is usually fruit-flavored and sometimes contains gelatin.
- **Frozen yogurt** uses yogurt to replace some of the milk or cream, giving the dessert a tartness. Yogurt complements fruit flavors.
- **Sorbet** does not contain milk. It contains pureed fruit or fruit juices with very intense flavors.
- **Ice** is sorbet with a more granular texture.

INGREDIENTS

The secret to making great ice cream is to use the highest quality ingredients you can find. As the ice cream melts on the tongue, defects are readily noticeable.

VANILLA EXTRACT

Heading the list is the ubiquitous vanilla extract. Use only the highest quality pure vanilla extract. The cost difference per quart of ice cream is only pennies, but the taste difference is remarkable.

CHOCOLATE AND COCOA

Often unsweetened cocoa is better in chocolate-flavored ice creams than solid chocolate. Buy a high-quality Dutch process cocoa and heat it with the sugar or corn syrup to develop and distribute full flavor. When you use solid chocolate, be sure to melt it slowly and to combine it completely with warm liquid before chilling. This will prevent the chocolate from clumping and leaving little bits of undissolved chocolate in your ice cream. Whirring the mix in a blender will help to better combine the chocolate. If you suspect lumps, pass the mix through a fine sieve when you pour it into the freezer container.

SWEETENERS

We like cane sugar to sweeten ice cream. It has received less processing and isn't as likely to have "off" flavors as is sugar derived from beets or other sources. If you are going to assemble the mix in a blender or food processor, regular granulated sugar is fine. If you just stir the mix with a spoon, use superfine sugar, which dissolves easier. In recipes calling for brown sugar, we like dark brown cane sugar. For sherbets and sorbets, we like to use light corn syrup. It produces a nicer texture than granulated sugar. Some recipes call for you to dissolve sugar in water to make a simple syrup, which is slightly sweeter than light corn syrup and doesn't produce quite as nice a texture. Honey can be used, but we find that the flavor dominates other flavoring added to the mix. If you really like honey, try making a vanilla mix sweetened with honey.

We have used NutraSweet, which is the dietetic sweetener found in Equal, in a few recipes. The taste is fine, but the frozen product isn't nearly as smooth as it would be if you used sugar or corn syrup. If your diet restricts sugar intake, ice cream made with NutraSweet makes an acceptable substitute for the real thing.

NUTS

Chopped nuts are wonderful when added to an ice cream mix or served over frozen ice cream. Buy the freshest nuts available, and if they are not already toasted, put them on a cookie sheet in a 350° oven for a few minutes. Shake the cookie sheet occasionally to prevent burning. Remove the nuts from the oven when they begin to release the fragrance of toasted nuts. Allow to cool, and chop coarsely before adding to the almost frozen mix.

EGGS

When we were kids, our parents added raw eggs or egg yolks to ice cream mix without giving it a second thought. With the recent documented cases of salmonella-induced illness, we must now be prudent in the use of raw eggs. Care must even be taken with cooked custard ice cream. The classic "cook until mixture coats the back of a spoon" instructions are not adequate to totally eliminate salmonella problems. The custard must reach and maintain a temperature of 130° for no less than 3 minutes, or be heated to a temperature of 160° before being chilled, to be free of the salmonella bacteria.

As with all ingredients, freshness is very important in eggs. Buy your eggs only from a store that does a volume business in eggs and refrigerates them. Always store your eggs in the refrigerator, and buy only the quantity that you will use in a week or 10 days. If an egg is cracked or dirty, discard it.

Fortunately, in recent years several products have come on the market that help alleviate the uncooked egg problem. These are the "egg substitutes," which are pasteurized and, therefore, bacteria-free. They can be added to a mix without cooking and then frozen without concern. Some of these products consist mainly of egg whites and are totally fat-free. Other products replace the yolks with an unsaturated, cholesterol-free fat. The product that we used most in testing these recipes is Egg Beaters. It comes in a convenient

4-ounce container, just the right amount for a 1-quart ice cream recipe, and helps produce a better texture without adding any fat or cholesterol. All the recipes calling for egg substitutes work well with Egg Beaters, but using a substitute with fat will produce a richer, creamier ice cream that is higher in calories.

MILK AND CREAM

The butterfat content of milk and cream varies, not only from region to region, but also from producer to producer within the same region. The most consistent is nonfat or skim milk, which is legally required to have less than ½ percent butterfat, but may have dried milk solids added to give it some body and keep it from looking so "blue" in the glass. Extra low fat milk has about 1 percent butterfat and 11 percent milk solids. Low fat milk or "two percent ten" has about 2 percent butterfat and 10 percent milk solids. Whole milk has about 3½ percent butterfat and 8 percent milk solids, but this can vary widely depending on the breed of cow, the feed that it receives and the dairy that bottles it. Half-and-half has about 10 percent butterfat. Light cream is next (about 20 percent butterfat), then light whipping cream (about 30 percent), then heavy cream (about 40 percent). We tested these recipes using extra low fat milk. Any of the recipes can be made richer by using a richer type of milk or cream, enhancing the texture and creaminess. Conversely, recipes can be made leaner, but you will give up something in texture, and the result will be a grainier product.

BUTTERMILK

Before yogurt became commonly available, many homemade ice cream recipes called for buttermilk. Real churned buttermilk has flecks of butterfat and adds richness as well as tartness to a frozen dessert. While neither of us is especially fond of buttermilk as a drink, we do like the taste of ice cream made with buttermilk and have included several recipes that use it. Again, use the buttermilk that you prefer in your ice cream: cultured, churned, with or without some butterfat.

YOGURT

In testing the desserts that call for yogurt and drained yogurt, we used every brand of yogurt available in our local supermarkets. We were amazed at the wide variation in texture, creaminess and acidity. Some were made from whole milk. Others had nonfat dry milk added to skim milk to make a more full-bodied product. Some added tapioca or other starch or gelatin to produce a thicker product. The tartness of the yogurts varied widely, and those with "active cultures" seemed to get even more tart as they approached their "use by" dates. Yogurts made from whole milk produce a smoother, creamier frozen dessert, just as frozen desserts made with half-and-half are smoother than those made with plain milk. Let your conscience and dietary restrictions be your guides. Fruit-flavored frozen yogurts are especially delicious. The tartness of the yogurt perks up the flavor of the fruit. If yogurt weren't used, it would often be necessary to add lemon juice. Plain yogurt, whether it is homemade or commercially produced, contains a lot of whey, which is basically just mildly acidic water with a slight bitterness. The whey adds little to the character of frozen yogurt. Fortunately, it is very easy to drain much of the whey from yogurt. All you need is a yogurt strainer, which can be inexpensively purchased in house-wares departments or gourmet specialty stores. If you don't have a yogurt strainer, the old method of lining a strainer with several layers of damp cheesecloth or a coffee filter works well. In a pinch you can even use an old tea towel or an old T-shirt. After it is drained, yogurt is thicker and will yield a creamier, more nutritious frozen dessert.

DRAINED YOGURT

Place a pint of plain, natural yogurt, homemade or commercial, in a strainer suspended over a measuring cup or bowl. The yogurt should not contain gelatin or added starch. There should be enough room in the receiving container to hold a cup of liquid without touching the strainer. Cover with an inverted plastic bag and put in the refrigerator for 8 hours or overnight. Depending on the yogurt used, the volume will reduce to about half, or 16 ounces yogurt will yield about 1 cup drained yogurt.

FRUITS AND BERRIES

Nothing is better than seasonal fruits, picked at the peak of perfection. The season is short for most fruits and berries, so find an excuse to make a frozen dessert from them while they are at their finest. If you get a yearning for fresh peach ice cream in February, however, the frozen peach slices that are sold in 16-ounce bags serve as a wonderful substitute for fresh fruit. This is also true for strawberries, raspberries, blackberries, cherries and blueberries. While it is still frozen, the fruit can be placed in a blender or food processor along with the milk or other liquid in the recipe and processed until smooth. Add remaining ingredients, process to combine and pour immediately into the ice cream freezer container.

ICE CREAM MAKERS

Old-fashioned hand-cranked ice cream makers are still available, in capacities ranging from 1 quart to several gallons. Purists insist that hand-cranked ice cream is better than that made in a motor-driven machine. We believe that if there is any difference at all, it is very slight. At least one company makes the same freezer in both hand-cranked and electric models. The more expensive freezers have wooden tubs, which are very durable and offer some insulation for the melting ice. The mix is placed in a freezer can that is immersed in the melting ice. The crank or motor turns the can around a stationary dasher that scrapes the newly frozen mix from the sides of the rotating can. There are less expensive models that have fiberglass or plastic tubs. All produce a smooth, creamy frozen dessert.

A newer innovation utilizes a sealed, coolant-filled canister that is put in the freezer for several hours. When it is very cold, chilled ice cream mix is then placed in the container. As the mixture freezes on the sides of the container, it is scraped off by a rotating paddle. The original freezers of this type were hand-cranked, but motorized models have been introduced recently. The ice cream is almost as smooth and creamy as that made in the old-fashioned-type freezer. Most of these makers have a capacity of a little over 1 quart.

The most expensive makers have built-in chilling units. All that is necessary is to pour in the chilled ice cream mix and turn on the machine. The ice cream is very good, but the main advantage of these machines is convenience. This type usually has a capacity of a little over 1 quart, also.

Regardless of the type of machine you use, follow the manufacturer's instructions for freezing frozen desserts.

SALT

If your ice cream maker uses salt to melt ice, you have some choice as to the type of salt you use. If you don't have rock (or "ice cream") salt, you can always use kosher salt or even table salt.

ICE

The best ice to use in an old-fashioned freezer is ice crushed in pieces about the size of marbles. Some manufacturers call for ice cubes, which is very convenient if your refrigerator is equipped with an automatic ice maker. Layer ice and salt. A good rule of thumb is to use

1 part salt to 12 parts ice. We save ½-gallon milk containers, fill them with water and freeze them. When they are solidly frozen it only takes a couple of firm taps with a hammer on each side to shatter the ice into small pieces. You can then pour the crushed ice into the freezer tub. Three ½-gallon containers and a cup of salt are more than enough to make a full quart of frozen dessert.

HELPFUL HINTS

Most recipes containing eggs and cream call for a "dash" of salt. Many people are cutting down on their salt intake, and the salt can be totally omitted if desired. A little salt does pick up the flavor of many frozen desserts. A dash is about ⅛ teaspoon; you should certainly not use more than ¼ teaspoon for a 1-quart frozen dessert recipe.

Some recipes call for a "pinch" of salt or other ingredient. A pinch is about ¹⁄₁₆ teaspoon.

We found that the frozen juice concentrates, used undiluted, have strong, pure flavors and make easy, economical frozen desserts. We have used several in our recipes. Feel free to substitute if you have a family favorite.

Likewise, canned nectars and juices are great basic ingredients. They have a good acid-fruit balance and a strong fruit flavor.

For coffee-flavored desserts, we found that a good instant espresso coffee added a very pleasant coffee flavor without taking time to brew extra strong coffee and allow it to cool.

We have added liqueurs or other alcoholic beverages to several recipes. They help carry the flavor of the dessert, but if you can taste alcohol, you have added too much. Triple Sec is especially nice in fruit-flavored desserts. Orange juice and a little grated orange peel can be substituted. If you add more than ¼ cup alcohol per quart of mixture, it won't freeze right and will remain slushy.

We have added nonfat dry milk to many of our recipes. This doesn't add any fat, and helps smooth out the finished dessert. Too much dried milk tends to make the dessert gummy and taste dull. We find nonfat dry milk to be much better than evaporated milk, which always has a strange "cooked" taste.

We tend to like frozen desserts that are less sweet than most commercial products. If you like sweeter desserts, add more sugar or corn syrup. You can also add a packet or two of Equal to the recipe as written. This will make the dessert taste sweeter without adding calories.

We found a heavy duty blender to be very effective in mixing recipes. The ingredients can be added directly to the blender container, blended until thoroughly combined and then chilled in the blender container. Just before pouring into the ice cream freezer, whir for a few seconds to recombine the ingredients and to incorporate a little air into the mixture, which will lighten the ice cream. If you don't have a blender, a food processor works almost as well.

Homemade frozen desserts are at their best when served straight from the ice cream maker. They will keep for a few days in the freezer, but larger ice crystals develop and the desserts become grainier. Freeze in a plastic microwave-safe container. Just from the freezer, desserts tend to be very hard and not at all smooth. If they are allowed to mellow in the refrigerator for 30 minutes, they will be smooth and more manageable. Alternately, you can put the container in the microwave for a minute or two on DEFROST. This will make the dessert easier to serve and improve the texture.

You are ready to start making homemade desserts. We have included a wide variety of recipes and hope you will find a few that really please you.

RICH AND CREAMY

ALMOND PRALINE ICE CREAM

*Make **Almond Praline**, page 17, before you start the ice cream, and crush it into a fine powder. This ice cream is delicious served with some fresh sliced strawberries or peaches.*

2¾ cups half-and-half
¼ cup sugar
pinch salt
3 eggs

¾ cup *Almond Praline* powder
2 tsp. vanilla extract
⅛ tsp. almond extract

Combine half-and-half, sugar and salt in a small saucepan. Heat until bubbles start to form around the edge and mixture is quite warm. Whisk eggs in a small bowl. Carefully add a few spoonfuls of hot cream mixture to eggs to gradually warm them. Pour egg mixture back into saucepan and continue to cook over low heat until custard thickens slightly and reaches 160° on a candy thermometer. Remove from heat; pour through a strainer into a small bowl set in another bowl of cold or ice water. Stir in praline powder, vanilla and almond extract. When cool, cover and chill in the refrigerator until ready to freeze. Pour into the ice cream maker and follow the manufacturer's instructions for freezing.

ALMOND PRALINE

*Make this ahead of time and keep in an airtight container. Sprinkle it on top of ice cream or sundaes, or use it in as an ingredient in ice cream. Substitute chopped pecans for almonds to make **Pecan Praline**.*

1 tsp. vegetable oil
½ cup sugar
2 tbs. water

½ cup blanched slivered almonds or
    pecans, lightly toasted

Lightly oil a cookie sheet or a large piece of foil with vegetable oil. Combine sugar and water in a small heavy saucepan. Cook over medium low heat without stirring until sugar melts and turns a light golden brown. Pour in nuts, tipping saucepan to cover nuts with caramel mixture as much as possible. The caramel mixture will turn dark very quickly, so continue to cook for another minute or two just until nuts and syrup turn a dark golden brown. Immediately pour nuts and syrup out on oiled cookie sheet or foil and allow to cool. As soon as praline is cool, break into pieces and process in a food processor or blender. If using as a topping, process until pieces are quite small. If adding to an ice cream mixture before freezing, process to a powder. Praline will absorb moisture at room temperature, so store it in an airtight container immediately after crushing.

CHOCOLATE PECAN PRALINE ICE CREAM

Makes: about 1 quart

*Nuggets of pecan give this luscious chocolate ice cream a little crunch. Make **Pecan Praline** by using the recipe for **Almond Praline**, page 17, substituting chopped pecans for almonds. Make it ahead and keep tightly covered.*

1 cup milk
1/3 cup unsweetened cocoa
2 cups half-and-half
1/4 cup dark corn syrup
4 oz. Egg Beaters, or egg substitute

2 tbs. nonfat dry milk
2 tsp. vanilla extract
dash salt
3/4 cup *Pecan Praline*

Heat milk with cocoa in a small saucepan until cocoa dissolves. Remove from heat and place saucepan in a bowl of cold or ice water to cool mixture. Pour into a blender or food processor and add remaining ingredients, except *Pecan Praline*. Process until smooth. Cover and refrigerate until ready to freeze. Pour mixture into the ice cream maker, add *Pecan Praline* and follow the manufacturer's instructions for freezing.

EASY CARAMEL ICE CREAM

Makes: about 1 quart

Leftover caramel ice cream sauce makes a delicious quick ice cream. A drizzle of chocolate sauce adds a nice touch.

¾ cup *Caramel Sauce*, page 116
4 oz. Egg Beaters, or egg substitute
2½ cups half-and-half
⅓ cup nonfat dry milk
1 tsp. vanilla extract
dash salt

Heat *Caramel Sauce* slightly so it will pour into a blender or food processor. Add remaining ingredients and process until smooth. Chill in the refrigerator until ready to freeze. Blend for a few seconds before pouring into the ice cream maker. Follow the manufacturer's instructions for freezing.

HAZELNUT GELATO

Makes: about 1 quart

Toast hazelnuts in a shallow pan in a 350° oven for 8 to 9 minutes, remove, place on a heavy towel and rub nuts vigorously in the towel to remove brown skins.

1 cup toasted hazelnuts, as many skins
    removed as possible
2 cups half-and-half
2 eggs
2 egg yolks

⅔ cup dark corn syrup
2 tbs. Frangelico, or brandy
1 tbs. vanilla extract
dash salt

Process nuts in a food processor or blender until very fine. Heat half-and-half in a small saucepan until bubbles form around the edge and mixture is quite warm. Beat eggs and egg yolks together in a small bowl. Carefully add about ½ cup hot cream mixture, a spoonful at a time, into eggs to gradually warm them. Return eggs to cream in saucepan and continue cooking over low heat, stirring constantly until mixture forms a custard and reaches 160° on a candy thermometer. Remove saucepan from heat and place in another bowl of cold or ice water to cool mixture to lukewarm. Pour through a strainer into a blender or food processor; add remaining ingredients. Process until smooth. Cover and refrigerate until ready to freeze. Follow the manufacturer's instructions for freezing.

20 RICH AND CREAMY

CHOCOLATE GELATO

This Italian-style ice cream is smooth, creamy and very definitely chocolate. Part of the cream is whipped and folded in just before freezing the gelato.

1 tsp. plain unflavored gelatin
1/4 cup cold water
1 1/2 cups half-and-half
1 1/2 cups heavy cream
2 tsp. instant espresso coffee powder

1/2 cup sugar
3 oz. unsweetened chocolate, melted
1 tsp. vanilla extract
pinch salt

Soften gelatin in cold water. Heat half-and-half and 1/2 cup cream in a heavy saucepan over low heat until bubbles form around the edge. Do not boil. When cream is hot, sprinkle in coffee; add sugar and gelatin. Stir to dissolve gelatin and remove from heat. Whisk melted chocolate into hot cream; stir in vanilla and salt. Pour mixture through a strainer into a medium-sized bowl. Place saucepan in a pan of cold or ice water to cool mixture. Cover and chill in the refrigerator until ready to freeze. Whip remaining heavy cream until thick but not stiff, and gently fold into chilled mixture just before freezing. Pour mixture into the ice cream maker and follow the manufacturer's instructions for freezing.

WHITE CHOCOLATE COCONUT GELATO

Makes: about 1 quart

Toasted coconut folded into this ice cream adds a terrific flavor crunch.

2½ cups milk
⅓ cup sugar
pinch salt
4 oz. white chocolate
3 egg yolks

1 tsp. vanilla extract
½ cup sweetened flaked coconut,
  toasted in a 300° oven for
  10-12 minutes

Combine milk, sugar and salt in a heavy saucepan over low heat. Coarsely chop chocolate and add to saucepan. Cook over low heat until chocolate melts. Whisk egg yolks until thick and lemon-colored. Carefully add some of hot mixture to egg yolks to gradually warm them. Add egg yolks to saucepan and continue to cook over low heat until mixture thickens and reaches 160° on a candy thermometer, about 10 to 12 minutes. Remove from heat and add vanilla. Cool to room temperature, cover and chill in the refrigerator until ready to freeze. Pour into a blender or food processor and process for 10 seconds before filling the ice cream maker. Follow the manufacturer's instructions for freezing. When gelato is finished, stir in ¼ cup toasted coconut. Sprinkle remaining coconut on individual dishes just before serving.

IRISH COFFEE ICE CREAM

This is an appropriate dessert for St. Patrick's Day, or any time for coffee lovers.

1½ cups milk
2 tbs. instant espresso coffee powder
½ cup brown sugar
1¼ cups heavy cream
4 oz. Egg Beaters, or egg substitute
2 tsp. vanilla extract
¼ cup Irish whiskey, or brandy
dash salt

Combine milk, coffee and brown sugar in a small saucepan. Heat over low heat until sugar and coffee are dissolved. Remove from heat and place saucepan in another bowl of cold or ice water to cool mixture to room temperature. Pour milk mixture into a blender or food processor and add remaining ingredients. Blend until smooth. Cover and chill in the refrigerator until ready to freeze. Blend for a few seconds before pouring mixture into the ice cream maker. Follow the manufacturer's instructions for freezing.

MOCHA ALMOND FUDGE ICE CREAM

Makes: about 1 quart

A prepared chocolate fudge topping from the supermarket is folded into this wickedly rich ice cream.

¾ cup chopped toasted almonds
1 cup milk
4 oz. Egg Beaters, or egg substitute
⅔ cup sugar
1 tbs. instant espresso coffee powder

dash salt
1½ cups heavy cream
1 tsp. vanilla extract
½ cup chocolate fudge topping

Toast almonds in a 300° oven until lightly browned. Watch carefully to prevent burning, stirring occasionally. Allow to cool. Place milk, Egg Beaters, sugar, coffee and salt in a blender or food processor. Process until well combined. Add cream and vanilla. Cover and chill in the refrigerator until ready to freeze. Blend for a few seconds before pouring into the ice cream maker. Follow the manufacturer's instructions for freezing. When ice cream is frozen, add almonds just before removing from ice cream maker. Remove dasher and make a hole in the ice cream with the handle of a large wooden or metal spoon. Pour in fudge topping and swirl through ice cream with the spoon handle. Do not distribute too evenly, so there are pools of chocolate in the ice cream.

COFFEE ICE CREAM

*This is a terrific, creamy, intensely coffee-flavored dessert. Layer it in an ice cream cake or serve it in **Cookie Cups**, page 126.*

1 cup whole milk
⅔ cup sugar
2 egg yolks, lightly beaten
2 tbs. instant espresso coffee powder

1 tsp. vanilla extract
2 cups heavy cream
pinch salt

Heat milk in a small saucepan until bubbles form around the edge. Dissolve sugar in heated milk. Remove milk from heat and add 1 to 2 tablespoons hot milk to egg yolks to bring eggs gradually up to milk temperature. Add egg-milk mixture and coffee back to saucepan. Continue to cook over low heat, stirring constantly until mixture begins to thicken and reaches 160° on a candy thermometer. Place saucepan in a pan of cold or ice water and continue stirring to cool custard. When barely warm pour custard through a strainer into a bowl. Stir in vanilla, cream and salt. Chill in the refrigerator until ready to freeze. Pour into the ice cream maker and follow the manufacturer's instructions for freezing.

COGNAC ICE CREAM

This is a wonderful finish for a spicy dinner. Ice cream mix should be very cold before you start freezing it, because of the cognac. A dollop of chocolate sauce is a very nice accent.

2 cups heavy cream
1 cup milk
4 oz. Egg Beaters, or egg substitute
2/3 cup sugar
1 tsp. instant espresso coffee powder
1 tbs. vanilla extract
1/4 cup cognac, or brandy

Combine ingredients in a blender or food processor. Blend until smooth. Cover and chill in the refrigerator until ready to freeze. Pour into the ice cream maker and follow the manufacturer's instructions for freezing.

GERMAN CHOCOLATE PECAN ICE CREAM

Makes: about 1 quart

Sweetened coconut and chopped pecans add a texture crunch.

4 oz. German chocolate, melted
1 cup half-and-half
1 cup milk
⅓ cup sugar

2 eggs
1 tsp. vanilla extract
½ cup sweetened flaked coconut
½ cup toasted chopped pecans

Melt chocolate in the microwave on MEDIUM or in the top of a double boiler. In a medium saucepan over low heat, combine half-and-half, milk and sugar. Cook until bubbles form around the edge and mixture is warm to the touch. Whisk eggs in a small bowl and slowly add several spoonfuls of hot milk mixture to eggs to gradually warm them. Add eggs to saucepan and continue to cook over low heat, stirring constantly. Mixture will thicken slightly and reach a temperature of 160° on a candy thermometer. Stir in warm melted chocolate and vanilla. Place saucepan in a bowl of cold or ice water to cool mixture. Pour through a strainer into a blender, cover and process until well combined. Chill in the refrigerator until ready to freeze. Pour into the ice cream maker and follow the manufacturer's instructions for freezing. Just before ice cream is completely frozen, stir in coconut and pecans. Mix a little longer to combine ingredients.

MEXICAN CHOCOLATE ICE CREAM

Makes: about 1 quart

The sweet Mexican Ibarra chocolate with its blend of chocolate, almonds and cinnamon makes a delicious ice cream.

1 round (3.1 oz.) Ibarra chocolate, broken into 5-6 pieces
1½ cups half-and-half
1½ cups heavy cream
⅔ cup sugar
dash salt

Combine chocolate pieces with remaining ingredients in a small saucepan. Heat over low heat until chocolate and sugar dissolve. Remove from heat; place saucepan in a bowl of cold or ice water to cool. Cover and chill in the refrigerator until ready to freeze. Blend for a few seconds before pouring into the ice cream maker. Follow the manufacturer's instructions for freezing.

VARIATION

Make an ice cream cake using layers of *Rich Vanilla Custard Ice Cream*, page 46, *Mexican Chocolate Ice Cream* and *Easy Sponge Cake*, page 161.

OLD-FASHIONED CHOCOLATE ICE CREAM

Chocolate is one of the world's favorite ice cream flavors.

1 cup milk
2 cups heavy cream
½ cup sugar
2 egg yolks, beaten

2 oz. semisweet chocolate, melted
1 oz. unsweetened chocolate, melted
2 tsp. vanilla extract
dash salt

Combine milk and cream in a saucepan and heat over low heat until bubbles form around the edge and mixture is hot. Add sugar and stir to dissolve. Beat egg yolks in a small bowl and carefully add a few spoonfuls of hot cream mixture to eggs to gradually warm them. Stir eggs back into saucepan and continue to cook over low heat, stirring constantly, until mixture thickens slightly and reaches 160° on a candy thermometer. Remove from heat and strain custard into a bowl. Add chocolates, vanilla and salt. Place bowl in a pan of cold or ice water and cool to room temperature. Chill in the refrigerator until ready to freeze. Pour into the ice cream maker and follow the manufacturer's instructions for freezing.

SUPER CHOCOLATE ICE CREAM

Makes: about 1 quart

This intensely chocolate-flavored ice cream is a family favorite.

1/4 cup water
1/2 cup sugar
2 tbs. unsweetened cocoa
dash salt
6 oz. semisweet chocolate chips

3 cups half-and-half
2 tbs. nonfat dry milk
1 tbs. butter
2 tsp. vanilla extract

In the top of a double boiler over simmering water, combine water, sugar, cocoa and salt. Add chocolate chips and stir to melt. Over low heat in another saucepan, heat half-and-half, dry milk and butter until butter melts and mixture is very warm to the touch. Add to chocolate mixture and continue to cook over low heat until mixture is well combined and smooth. Remove from heat, add vanilla and cool to room temperature. Cover and chill in the refrigerator until ready to freeze. Pour mixture through a strainer into the ice cream maker and follow the manufacturer's instructions for freezing.

ROCKY ROAD ICE CREAM

Makes: about 1 quart

Add more nuts, marshmallows and chocolate chips to the ice cream if you like it really rocky.

2 cups heavy cream
1 cup half-and-half
⅓ cup sugar
dash salt
6 oz. milk chocolate, melted

4 oz. Egg Beaters, or egg substitute
2 tsp. vanilla extract
½ cup toasted chopped pecans
¼ cup miniature chocolate chips
½ cup miniature marshmallows

Heat cream, half-and-half, sugar and salt in a small saucepan until sugar dissolves. Add melted chocolate and stir to combine. Remove from heat and place in a pan of cold or ice water to cool to room temperature. Strain chocolate mixture into a blender or food processor; add Egg Beaters and vanilla. Process until smooth. Chill until ready to freeze. Pour into the ice cream maker and follow the manufacturer's instructions for freezing. About a minute before ice cream is finished, add nuts and chocolate chips and freeze for another minute. When ice cream is frozen, fold in marshmallows.

RICH STRAWBERRY ICE CREAM

Here is an old-fashioned, full-flavored strawberry ice cream. Serve a few sweet, sliced strawberries for garnish.

1½ cups fresh strawberries, stemmed,
   or 12 oz. frozen unsweetened strawberries
½ cup milk
1½ cups heavy cream
⅔ cup sugar
1 tbs. vanilla extract
2 tbs. Triple Sec, or orange-flavored liqueur
dash salt

Place strawberries in a blender or food processor and puree. Add remaining ingredients and process until smooth. Cover and refrigerate until ready to freeze. Blend for a few seconds before pouring into the ice cream maker. Follow the manufacturer's instructions for freezing.

SWEET CHERRY ICE CREAM

Use the luscious, fresh, black Bing cherries or the frozen, dark, sweet cherries to make this stunning ice cream.

3 cups fresh pitted Bing cherries, or
   1 pkg. (16 oz.) frozen dark sweet
   cherries, defrosted
4 oz. Egg Beaters, or egg substitute
1 cup half-and-half

$2/3$ cup superfine sugar
dash salt
1 tbs. lemon juice
2 tsp. vanilla extract
$1/2$ cup heavy cream

Place 2 cups pitted cherries in a blender or food processor with Egg Beaters, half-and-half, sugar and salt. Process until smooth. Add lemon juice, vanilla and cream. Process for 2 to 3 seconds until well blended. Chill in the refrigerator until ready to freeze. Coarsely chop remaining cup of cherries by hand. Cover and refrigerate. Pour mixture into the ice cream maker and follow the manufacturer's instructions for freezing. When ice cream is frozen, fold in reserved chopped cherries.

OLD-FASHIONED LEMON ICE CREAM

Makes: about 1 quart

Lemon is one of the world's best ice cream flavors. Garnish with fresh mint leaves or raspberries.

1 tsp. grated lemon peel
$\frac{1}{4}$ cup fresh lemon juice
1 cup sugar
4 oz. Egg Beaters, or egg substitute
$2\frac{1}{2}$ cups half-and-half
dash salt

Combine ingredients in a blender or food processor and process until smooth. Cover and refrigerate until ready to freeze. Pour into the ice cream maker and follow the manufacturer's instructions for freezing.

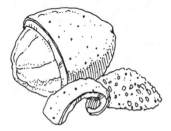

FROZEN ZABAGLIONE ICE CREAM

*The wonderful flavors of the well-known, frothy, hot, Marsala-laced sauce called zabaglione make a delicious ice cream. Garnish with a few toasted pine nuts or sliced strawberries, or serve with **Zinfandel Sauce**, page 120.*

2½ cups half-and-half
⅔ cup sugar
dash salt
3 eggs
¼ cup Marsala

Heat half-and-half, sugar and salt in a saucepan until sugar dissolves and there are bubbles around the edge. The mixture should be quite warm. Whisk eggs in a small bowl and carefully add a few spoonfuls of warm cream to eggs to gradually warm them. Pour eggs into saucepan and continue cooking over low heat, stirring constantly, until mixture starts to thicken and reaches 160° on a candy thermometer. Remove from heat, add Marsala and place saucepan in a pan of cold or ice water to cool mixture. Pour ice cream through a strainer into another bowl, cover and refrigerate until ready to freeze. Pour into the ice cream maker and follow the manufacturer's instructions for freezing.

CHESTNUT RUM ICE CREAM

If you are a chestnut fancier, try this ice cream. The chestnut and rum flavors make a terrific fall or holiday dessert. The chestnut spread is available in the fancy food section of most supermarkets. If only chestnut puree is available, increase the dark corn syrup to ⅔ cup.

1 can (8¾ oz.) chestnut spread
2 tbs. dark corn syrup
2 cups heavy cream
4 oz. Egg Beaters, or egg substitute
¼ cup dark rum
dash salt

Combine ingredients in a blender or food processor and blend until well combined. Cover and chill in the refrigerator until ready to freeze. Blend for a few seconds before pouring into the ice cream maker. Follow the manufacturer's instructions for freezing.

PISTACHIO NUT ICE CREAM

*Use unsalted roasted pistachios in this delicately green ice cream. This makes a delicious layer in **Rainbow Bombe**, page 166, or in a parfait.*

2 cups half-and-half
1 cup milk
4 oz. Egg Beaters, or egg substitute
2/3 cup sugar
2 tsp. vanilla extract
1/8 tsp. almond extract
dash salt
1-2 drops green food coloring, optional
1/2 cup coarsely chopped roasted pistachio nuts

Combine ingredients except pistachios in a blender or food processor and process until well combined. Cover and chill in the refrigerator until ready to freeze. Blend for a few seconds before pouring into the ice cream maker. Follow the manufacturer's instructions for freezing. About a minute before ice cream is finished, add nuts and finish freezing.

ORANGE COCONUT SHERBET

Creamy canned coconut milk is the base for this tropical-flavored sherbet.

1 cup frozen orange juice concentrate,
  partially defrosted
1 can (14 oz.) coconut milk
1/3 cup light corn syrup
1/2 cup milk
2 tbs. nonfat dry milk
2 tbs. Triple Sec, or orange-flavored liqueur
dash salt
1/2 cup sweetened flaked coconut

Combine ingredients except coconut in a blender or food processor and process until smooth. Cover and chill in the refrigerator until ready to freeze. Add coconut to mixture and blend for a few seconds before pouring into the ice cream maker. Coconut should be coarsely chopped but not smooth. Follow the manufacturer's instructions for freezing.

PEANUT BRITTLE ICE CREAM

Makes: about 1 quart

Salty, sweet peanuts make a delicious crunch either in or on top of this ice cream. Fold them in just before the ice cream is finished freezing.

2 (1.4 oz. each) Snicker's Munch Bars
3 cups half-and-half
2 tbs. nonfat dry milk
4 oz. Egg Beaters, or egg substitute
2/3 cup dark corn syrup
1 tsp. vanilla extract
dash salt

Lightly crush peanut brittle bars in their wrappers with a rolling pin or small mallet. Remove from wrappers, place in a small bowl and cover so peanut brittle doesn't absorb moisture from the air. Combine remaining ingredients in a blender or food processor and blend until well combined. Cover and refrigerate until ready to freeze. Blend for a few seconds before pouring into the ice cream maker. Follow the manufacturer's instructions for freezing. About a minute before ice cream is finished freezing, fold in crushed peanut brittle.

CREAMY PEANUT BUTTER ICE CREAM

Makes: about 1 quart

*This is good straight out of the ice cream maker, or serve it as an ice cream pie in a chocolate cookie crust or **Ginger Cookie Crust**, page 151.*

2 cups half-and-half
½ cup milk
½ cup nonfat dry milk
¾ cup peanut butter
¾ cup sugar
2 tsp. vanilla extract

In a medium saucepan, combine half-and-half, milk and dry milk. Cook over low heat to dissolve dry milk. Add peanut butter, stirring until smooth and creamy. Add sugar and cook until dissolved. Remove from heat; add vanilla. Cool slightly before covering and chilling mixture in the refrigerator. Blend for a few seconds before pouring into the ice cream maker. Follow the manufacturer's instructions for freezing.

PEPPERMINT PATTIE ICE CREAM

Makes: about 1 quart

Large chocolate-covered mints add a refreshing, minty flavor to this ice cream. If you really love peppermint, crush a few hard peppermint candies and sprinkle on top of each serving.

2 cups half-and-half
1 cup heavy cream
4 oz. Egg Beaters, or egg substitute
2 tbs. sugar
dash salt

3 (1.5 oz. each) chocolate-covered
 peppermint patties
1 tsp. vanilla extract
6 hard peppermint candies, crushed,
 optional

Combine half-and-half, cream, Egg Beaters, sugar and salt in a blender or food processor. Blend to combine. Cut peppermint patties into ½-inch chunks, add to blender with vanilla and process on HIGH until smooth. Cover and refrigerate until ready to freeze. Blend for a few seconds before pouring into the ice cream maker. Follow the manufacturer's instructions for freezing. Before unwrapping hard peppermint candies, hit each piece with a rolling pin or mallet to crush into small pieces. Do this at the last minute because candies will absorb moisture from the air and stick together.

RICH AND CREAMY 41

BUTTERSCOTCH ICE CREAM

Makes: about 1 quart

This is a luscious, rich, caramel-flavored ice cream.

3 tbs. butter
¾ cup dark brown sugar
¾ cup water
1 tsp. instant espresso coffee powder
2¼ cups half-and-half
¼ cup nonfat dry milk
1½ tsp. vanilla extract
dash salt

Melt butter in a small saucepan, add sugar and cook over low heat until sugar is dissolved. Add water, bring to a boil, add coffee and simmer for 1 to 2 minutes. Remove from heat and cool to room temperature. Pour into a blender or food processor and add remaining ingredients. Process until smooth. Cover and chill in the refrigerator until ready to freeze. Blend again for a few seconds before pouring into the ice cream maker. Follow the manufacturer's instructions for freezing.

HOLIDAY EGGNOG ICE CREAM

*If you like eggnog, you will love this spicy, creamy ice cream. Use eggnog straight out of the dairy case and flavor it with brandy, rum or whatever you like in eggnog. For an elegant dessert, use it for a layer in **Rainbow Bombe**, page 166.*

3 cups cold eggnog
2 tbs. brandy
generous amount grated nutmeg

Combine ingredients, pour into the ice cream maker and follow the manufacturer's instructions for freezing.

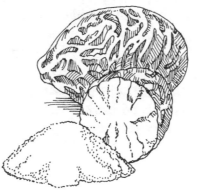

RASPBERRY VANILLA SWIRL ICE CREAM

*Make the **Raspberry Sauce**, page 117, ahead of time for this easy and pretty dessert. If you prefer, just spoon the sauce over rather than folding it into the ice cream.*

2 cups half-and-half
1 cup milk
2/3 cup sugar
1/2 cup nonfat dry milk

1 tbs. vanilla extract
1/8 tsp. lemon extract
dash salt
1/2-2/3 cup *Raspberry Sauce*

Combine ingredients except *Raspberry Sauce* in a blender or food processor and process until mixture is smooth. Cover and chill in the refrigerator until ready to freeze. Pour into the ice cream maker and follow the manufacturer's instructions for freezing. Ice cream should be quite firm when it is frozen; you can put it in the freezer to set up for about 30 minutes. Spoon ice cream out into a chilled bowl. Make a hole in the center of the ice cream with a thick spoon or spatula handle and pour in *Raspberry Sauce*. Starting at the center of the *Raspberry Sauce*, make a circle in the ice cream, dragging it into a swirl. Serve immediately.

PHILADELPHIA-STYLE VANILLA ICE CREAM

This is a classic vanilla ice cream that doesn't use eggs. If you have a 4- to 5-inch piece of vanilla bean, scrape the seeds into the cream mixture for a delicious flavor. Place the used vanilla bean in a small jar, cover with sugar and keep it in the cupboard. Use the sugar for making desserts.

1 cup heavy cream
2 cups half-and-half
seeds from a vanilla bean, or 1 tbs. vanilla extract
2/3 cup sugar
dash salt

Combine ingredients in a blender or food processor until sugar dissolves. Chill in the refrigerator until ready to freeze. Pour into the ice cream maker and follow the manufacturer's instructions for freezing.

RICH VANILLA CUSTARD ICE CREAM

Makes: about 1 quart

Vanilla ice cream is always a favorite, and this is an elegant, creamy version.

1 cup whole milk
½ cup sugar
dash salt
2 egg yolks, lightly beaten
2 cups heavy cream
2 tsp. vanilla extract

Place milk in a small saucepan and heat over low heat until bubbles form around the edge and mixture is hot. Add sugar and salt and stir to dissolve. Remove milk from heat and add 1 to 2 tbs. hot milk to egg yolks, mixing well. Continue to add a little more milk to egg yolks to bring eggs gradually up to milk temperature. Add egg-milk mixture back to saucepan and continue to cook over low heat, stirring constantly until it starts to thicken and reaches 160° on a candy thermometer, about 10 to 12 minutes. Place saucepan in a pan of cold or ice water and continue stirring to cool down custard. When custard is just barely warm, stir in cream and vanilla. Cover and chill in the refrigerator until ready to freeze. Pour mixture through a strainer into the ice cream maker and follow the manufacturer's instructions for freezing.

LIGHT AND LUSCIOUS

BLACKBERRY RHUBARB ICE CREAM

This intensely flavored ice cream is made with either fresh or frozen, un-sweetened blackberries and cooked rhubarb. It takes time to sieve the blackberries, but it is worth the effort to get a smooth ice cream. Pair scoops of this with orange sherbet and vanilla ice cream for a pretty and delicious dessert.

½ cup water
½ cup sugar
8 oz. rhubarb, trimmed and cut into
   1-inch pieces
16 oz. blackberries, fresh or defrosted

1 cup heavy cream
2 tbs. nonfat dry milk
¼ cup crème de cassis
dash salt

Combine water and sugar in a small saucepan and bring to a boil. Cook for 2 to 3 minutes until sugar is dissolved. Add rhubarb, cover and simmer for 3 to 4 minutes until fruit is tender. Remove saucepan from heat and place in a pan of cold or ice water to cool mixture. Puree blackberries in a blender or food processor with a little cream until smooth. Pour through a coarse strainer and press fruit through the sieve. Discard seeds. Return puree to blender or food processor with remaining ingredients; process until smooth. Cover and refrigerate until ready to freeze. Pour into the ice cream maker and follow the manufacturer's instructions for freezing.

DRIED CHERRY ICE CREAM

The small, tart, dried cherries add a great flavor punch to this kirsch-flavored ice cream.

2½ cups half-and-half
4 oz. Egg Beaters, or egg substitute
½ cup sugar
dash salt
1 tbs. vanilla extract
2 tbs. kirsch, or orange-flavored liqueur
¾ cup coarsely chopped dried cherries

Combine half-and-half, Egg Beaters, sugar, salt, vanilla, kirsch and ¼ cup dried cherries in a blender or food processor. Process until sugar is dissolved and mixture is smooth. Cover and chill in the refrigerator until ready to freeze. Pour into the ice cream maker and follow the manufacturer's instructions for freezing. About a minute before ice cream is frozen, add remaining ½ cup cherries to mixture and freeze for another minute.

FRESH PEACH ICE CREAM

Fresh summer peaches make a wonderful ice cream. Sprinkle with some fresh raspberries for color and flavor contrast.

2 cups half-and-half
3/4 cup sugar
1/4 cup nonfat dry milk
3 cups peeled pitted sliced peaches, or
  1 pkg. (16 oz.) frozen sliced peaches, defrosted
3 tbs. lemon juice
2 tsp. vanilla extract
dash salt

Combine half-and-half, sugar and dry milk in a blender or food processor and process until smooth. Add peaches with remaining ingredients and process until smooth. Chill in the refrigerator until ready to freeze. Blend mixture for a few seconds before pouring into the ice cream maker. Follow the manufacturer's instructions for freezing.

TANGERINE BUTTERMILK ICE CREAM

Makes: about 1 quart

*Fresh tangerine juice makes a pretty, light orange ice cream. This is particularly nice paired with **Raspberry Sherbet**, page 70, or a chocolate ice cream in **Cookie Cups**, page 126.*

1 cup tangerine juice (about 1¼ lb. before juicing)
1 cup buttermilk
1½ cups half-and-half
⅓ cup sugar
1 tbs. lemon juice
2 tbs. Triple Sec, or orange-flavored liqueur
dash salt

Combine ingredients in a blender or food processor and blend until smooth. Cover and chill in the refrigerator until ready to freeze. Blend for a few seconds before pouring into the ice cream maker. Follow the manufacturer's instructions for freezing.

HONEY ALMOND ICE CREAM

The flavor of honey really comes through in this ice cream. Use your favorite kind of honey. Very distinctive types produce a more pronounced honey taste.

2 cups half-and-half
1 cup milk
1/3 cup nonfat dry milk
4 oz. Egg Beaters, or egg substitute
1/2 cup honey
1 tsp. vanilla extract
1/8 tsp. almond extract
dash salt
1/2 cup toasted slivered almonds

Combine ingredients except almonds in a blender or food processor. Blend until smooth. Cover and chill in the refrigerator until ready to freeze. Blend for a few seconds before pouring into the ice cream maker. Follow the manufacturer's instructions for freezing. Either fold nuts into ice cream mixture about a minute before ice cream is done and continue to freeze for another minute, or sprinkle them over individual ice cream servings.

ORANGE WALNUT ICE CREAM

*Toasted walnuts are folded into this creamy ice cream at the very end of the freezing operation. For company, serve in **Lace Cookies**, page 125, made into cookie cups, or make an ice cream pie with a chocolate cookie crust.*

½ cup frozen orange juice concentrate,
   partially defrosted
1 cup buttermilk
2 cups half-and-half
½ cup light corn syrup

2 tbs. Triple Sec, or orange-flavored
   liqueur
2 tbs. nonfat dry milk
dash salt
½ cup toasted chopped walnuts

Combine ingredients except nuts in a blender or food processor and process until well combined. Cover and refrigerate until ready to freeze. Blend for a few seconds before pouring into the ice cream maker. Follow the manufacturer's instructions for freezing. About a minute before ice cream is frozen, add nuts and finish freezing.

VARIATION

Add ½ cup toasted flaked coconut instead of walnuts.

SUGAR-FREE BLACK WALNUT ICE CREAM

Makes: about 1 quart

Black walnuts add a very distinctive flavor to this ice cream, but toasted, chopped pecans or hazelnuts are delicious, too.

3 cups half-and-half
4 oz. Egg Beaters, or egg substitute
5 tsp. NutraSweet sweetener
1 tbs. vanilla extract
1/8 tsp. black walnut extract, or 2-3 drops almond extract
dash salt
1/2 cup finely chopped black walnuts

Combine all ingredients except nuts in a food processor or blender. Process until smooth. Cover and chill in the refrigerator until ready to freeze. Pour into the ice cream maker and follow the manufacturer's instructions for freezing. About a minute before ice cream is frozen, add nuts and continue freezing until ice cream is done.

LEMON CHEESECAKE ICE CREAM

If you like cheesecake, this ice cream is for you. Fresh strawberries or raspberries make a delicious and pretty garnish. This makes an elegant ice cream pie with either a chocolate cookie crust or **Graham Cracker Cookie Crust**, *page 152.*

2 cups milk
1 pkg. (8 oz.) light cream cheese (Neufchâtel)
½ cup sugar
3 tbs. Triple Sec, or orange-flavored liqueur
1 tsp. vanilla extract
½ tsp. lemon extract
dash salt

Place all ingredients in a blender or food processor and process until very smooth. Chill until ready to freeze. Pour into the ice cream maker and follow the manufacturer's instructions for freezing.

LEMON TEA ICE CREAM

This is a refreshing, lemon-flavored ice cream to serve after a summer lunch. Garnish with a few fresh mint leaves.

3 cups half-and-half
½ cup sugar
6 lemon tea bags
4 oz. Egg Beaters, or egg substitute
dash salt

In a small saucepan, bring 1 cup half-and-half and sugar almost to a boil. Add tea bags, cover, remove from heat and allow to steep for about 20 minutes. Remove tea bags, pressing out as much liquid as possible. When tea mixture has cooled, pour into a blender or food processor. Add remaining half-and-half, Egg Beaters and salt. Process for a few seconds until smooth. Cover and chill until ready to freeze. Pour into the ice cream maker and follow the manufacturer's instructions for freezing.

PINEAPPLE GINGER ICE CREAM

Fresh ginger adds a delightful flavor to this pineapple ice cream.

⅓ cup water
½ cup sugar
1 tbs. finely chopped peeled ginger root
1 cup frozen pineapple juice concentrate,
    defrosted
1 cup half-and-half
1½ cups buttermilk
½ tsp. grated lemon peel
dash salt

Combine water, sugar and ginger in a small saucepan. Bring to a boil and cook for 3 to 4 minutes until sugar is dissolved and ginger releases its flavor. Place saucepan in another bowl of cold or ice water to cool mixture to room temperature. Strain sugar and ginger mixture into a blender or food processor. Add remaining ingredients and blend until smooth. Cover and chill until ready to freeze. Pour into the ice cream maker and follow the manufacturer's instructions for freezing.

CINNAMON CANDY ICE CREAM

The little cinnamon Red Hots make a gorgeous pink, spicy cinnamon ice cream. Make it for your valentine or for a child's birthday party.

1 cup milk
3/4 cup sugar
1/4 cup (2 oz.) Red Hots, or cinnamon candies
dash salt
2 cups half-and-half
1/2 cup nonfat dry milk
1 1/2 tsp. vanilla extract

Place milk, sugar, Red Hots and salt in a small heavy saucepan. Cook over low heat, stirring constantly until candies melt, about 10 to 12 minutes. Remove from heat and allow to cool to room temperature. Pour candy mixture into a blender or food processor with half-and-half, dry milk and vanilla. Process until smooth. Chill in the refrigerator until ready to freeze. Blend for a few seconds before pouring mixture into the ice cream maker. Follow the manufacturer's instructions for freezing.

CREAM SHERRY ICE CREAM

Sweet sherry makes a subtly flavored ice cream. Top with toasted pecans or almonds for a crunchy texture.

¾ cup cream sherry
⅓ cup dark corn syrup
4 oz. Egg Beaters, or egg substitute
¼ cup nonfat dry milk
2 cups half-and-half
2 tsp. vanilla extract
pinch grated nutmeg
dash salt

Combine ingredients in a blender or food processor and blend until well combined. Cover and chill in the refrigerator until ready to freeze. Blend for a few seconds before pouring into the ice cream maker. Follow the manufacturer's instructions for freezing.

CREAMY CHOCOLATE YOGURT

Makes: about 1 quart

This tangy dessert is for chocolate lovers!

¾ cup whole milk
1 tsp. plain gelatin
⅔ cup sugar
dash salt
2 oz. semisweet chocolate, coarsely chopped
2½ cups plain yogurt
2 tsp. vanilla extract

Place milk in a small saucepan. Soften gelatin in milk. Slowly heat milk to dissolve gelatin. Add sugar, salt and chocolate. Stir over low heat until smooth, but do not boil. Remove from heat and place saucepan in a pan of cold or ice water to cool, or allow to cool at room temperature. Whisk in yogurt and vanilla. Chill mixture in the refrigerator until ready to freeze. Blend for a few seconds before pouring through a strainer into the ice cream maker. Follow the manufacturer's instructions for freezing.

EASY CHOCOLATE MALTED ICE CREAM

Makes: about 1 quart

One burger place in Southern California used to serve a thick, wonderful malted ice cream like this in tall, silver malt cups with long spoons.

1 small can (5.5 oz.) Hershey's Chocolate Syrup
2½ cups half-and-half
4 oz. Egg Beaters, or egg substitute
⅓ cup malted milk powder
¼ cup sugar
dash salt
1 tsp. vanilla extract

Combine chocolate syrup, half-and-half and Egg Beaters in a blender. Process until well mixed. Add remaining ingredients and blend until milk powder and sugar are dissolved. Chill in the refrigerator until ready to freeze. Blend for a few seconds before pouring into the ice cream maker. Follow the manufacturer's instructions for freezing.

RICE AND RAISIN ICE CREAM

Makes: about 1 quart

Soft, cooked rice gives this ice cream an extra rich taste and texture. The rice can be cooked ahead and refrigerated until you are ready to make the ice cream.

1³⁄₄ cups water
dash salt
¹⁄₂ cup long grain rice
2 tbs. dark rum
³⁄₄ cup golden or dark raisins
2 cups half-and-half
²⁄₃ cup sugar
2 eggs
2 tsp. vanilla extract

Place water and salt in a small saucepan and bring to a boil. Add rice, cover and lower heat. Cook over very low heat for about 30 minutes. Rice will be very soft and most of water absorbed. Remove from heat and allow to cool. Warm rum in a small saucepan and add raisins. Remove from heat and allow raisins to soften. Make a custard by heating half-and-half and sugar in a small saucepan until bubbles form around the edge and mixture is warm to the touch. Whisk eggs in a small bowl and gradually add several spoonfuls of hot cream-sugar mixture to eggs to warm them. Add eggs to remaining hot mixture and continue to cook over low heat, stirring constantly, until mixture thickens slightly and reaches 160° on a candy thermometer. Remove from heat. Place saucepan in a larger bowl of cold or ice water to cool mixture to almost room temperature. Pour custard through a strainer into a blender or food processor. Add cooked rice and process on HIGH until mixture is smooth. Add vanilla and any remaining rum in the bottom of raisin bowl. Chill in the refrigerator until ready to freeze. Blend for a few seconds before pouring into the ice cream maker. Follow the manufacturer's instructions for freezing. When ice cream is almost frozen, stir in raisins and continue to freeze for another minute to combine.

SPICY PUMPKIN ICE CREAM

Makes: about 1 quart

*This ice cream has all the wonderful flavors of a good pumpkin pie. Serve it with sugar cookies, or use to fill a **Ginger Cookie Crust**, page 151.*

½ cup canned or cooked pumpkin
⅓ cup (6 oz.) Egg Beaters, or egg substitute
½ cup sugar
¼ cup brown sugar
½ cup nonfat dry milk
2 cups half-and-half
¼ tsp. cinnamon
¼ tsp. ground ginger
⅛ tsp. grated nutmeg
dash salt

Combine all ingredients in a blender or food processor. Process until smooth. Chill in the refrigerator until ready to freeze. Pour mixture through a strainer into the ice cream maker and follow the manufacturer's instructions for freezing.

PUMPKIN PECAN ICE CREAM

*Pumpkin, pecans and a little rum make a great fall dessert. Try layering this in a parfait with ginger cookie crumbs and **Caramel Sauce**, page 116.*

1 cup half-and-half
1 cup heavy cream
1 cup canned pumpkin
1/2 cup nonfat dry milk
2/3 cup dark corn syrup

3 tbs. dark rum
2 tsp. vanilla extract
1/2 tsp. allspice
dash salt
3/4 cup toasted chopped pecans

Combine half-and-half, cream and pumpkin in a blender or food processor. Process until smooth. Add remaining ingredients except pecans and process until well combined. Chill in the refrigerator until ready to freeze. Blend for a few seconds before pouring into the ice cream maker. Follow the manufacturer's instructions for freezing. A minute or two before ice cream is frozen, stir in nuts and continue freezing for another minute to combine ingredients.

VANILLA FROZEN YOGURT

Drain some yogurt the night before making this ice cream (see page 8). This is delicious with any fresh sliced fruit or raspberries.

1 cup drained yogurt
1 cup half-and-half
1 cup milk
⅔ cup sugar
4 oz. Egg Beaters, or egg substitute
1 tbs. vanilla extract
dash salt

Combine ingredients in a blender or food processor and blend until smooth. Cover and chill in the refrigerator until ready to freeze. Blend mixture for a few seconds before pouring into the ice cream maker. Follow the manufacturer's instructions for freezing.

BANANA NUT ICE CREAM

Use really ripe bananas to bring out the most intense, sweet banana flavor in this ice cream.

2 large or 3 small very ripe bananas,
  slightly mashed (about 1½ cups)
2 cups half-and-half
⅓ cup sugar
2 tbs. lemon juice
1 tsp. vanilla extract
dash salt
½ cup toasted chopped pecans, walnuts or almonds

Place bananas, half-and-half and sugar in a blender or food processor. Process on HIGH until very smooth. Stir in lemon juice, vanilla and salt. Process to combine. Chill in the refrigerator until ready to freeze. Blend for a few seconds before pouring into the ice cream maker. Follow the manufacturer's instructions for freezing. A minute or two before ice cream is frozen, stir in nuts and continue to freeze for another minute to combine ingredients.

DELICIOUSLY LOW FAT

RASPBERRY SHERBET

This delicious sherbet has a light touch of orange flavoring.

2 pkg. (10 oz. each) frozen raspberries,
  defrosted
1½ cups milk
⅓ cup nonfat dry milk
2 tbs. Triple Sec, or orange juice

Puree defrosted raspberries in a blender or food processor until smooth. Pour mixture through a strainer, pressing out as much fruit pulp as possible. Discard seeds. Place raspberry puree back in blender or food processor with remaining ingredients and process until well combined. Chill in the refrigerator until ready to freeze. Pour into the ice cream maker and follow the manufacturer's instructions for freezing.

BLUEBERRY SHERBET

Pair this with a scoop each of raspberry sherbet and vanilla ice cream for a patriotic holiday dessert.

1 pkg. (16 oz.) frozen blueberries, partially
  defrosted, or 2 cups fresh blueberries,
  stemmed and washed
1½ cups milk
¾ cup light corn syrup
3 tbs. lime juice
2 tbs. Triple Sec, or orange-flavored liqueur

Combine blueberries, milk, corn syrup and lime juice in a blender or food processor. Process until smooth. Pour mixture through a strainer, pressing out all juice. Discard skins. Add Triple Sec to strained mixture, cover and refrigerate until ready to freeze. Pour into the ice cream maker and follow the manufacturer's instructions for freezing.

GRAPE YOGURT SHERBET

This easy, low fat sherbet starts with frozen grape juice concentrate. Use low fat yogurt for this sherbet. Remember to start draining the yogurt the night before (see page 8).

1 cup drained yogurt
1 can (12 oz.) sweetened frozen grape
  juice concentrate, partially defrosted
¼ cup nonfat dry milk
1¼ cups low fat milk
⅓ cup corn syrup

Combine ingredients in a blender or food processor and blend until smooth. Cover and chill until ready to freeze. Blend for a few seconds before pouring into the ice cream maker. Follow the manufacturer's instructions for freezing.

PRUNE AND BRANDY YOGURT

Sweet dried prunes make a luscious, creamy, low fat dessert. If the prunes are very hard and dry, simmer them in the heated milk for 15 to 20 minutes before blending.

1½ cups whole milk
½ cup nonfat dry milk
⅓ cup sugar
¾ cup soft pitted prunes, cut into ½-inch pieces
2 tbs. brandy, or cognac, optional
1 tsp. vanilla extract
1½ cups plain yogurt
dash salt

Pour milks and sugar in a blender or food processor. Process until well mixed. Add prunes and process on HIGH until smooth. Add remaining ingredients, blending until well combined. Chill in blender container or bowl in the refrigerator until ready to freeze. Blend for a few seconds before pouring mixture into the ice cream freezer. Follow the manufacturer's instructions for freezing.

BLACKBERRY FROZEN YOGURT

Fresh or frozen blackberries make a beautiful, dark, creamy yogurt. The drained yogurt (see page 8) makes all the difference in this dessert. Make it the night before; it will also keep for several days in the refrigerator.

1 pkg. (16 oz.) frozen blackberries, defrosted, or 3 cups fresh blackberries, stemmed and washed
1/3 cup sugar
1/3 cup water

1 cup low fat or skim milk
1 cup drained yogurt
1/2 cup nonfat dry milk
2 tbs. black currant liqueur, or Triple Sec or orange juice

Process blackberries in a blender or food processor. Place in a strainer and push through juice and fruit, discarding seeds. In a small saucepan, combine sugar and water. Bring to a boil, lower heat and cook for 3 to 4 minutes to dissolve sugar. Remove from heat and allow to cool, or place saucepan in a larger bowl of cold or ice water. Combine cooled sugar mixture, blackberry puree and remaining ingredients in blender or food processor. Process until smooth and creamy. Chill in the refrigerator until ready to freeze. Blend for a few seconds before pouring into the ice cream maker. Follow the manufacturer's instructions for freezing.

STRAWBERRY RHUBARB YOGURT

Makes: about 1 quart

Strawberries and rhubarb are a wonderful springtime combination. Garnish with fresh sliced strawberries. Start draining the yogurt the night before making this dessert (see page 8).

²/₃ cup water
²/₃ cup sugar
½ lb. fresh rhubarb, trimmed, cut into 1-inch pieces
1 pt. fresh strawberries, stemmed and washed
3 tbs. nonfat dry milk
½ cup half-and-half
1 cup drained yogurt

Combine water and sugar in a small saucepan. Bring to a boil, add rhubarb pieces, cover and simmer for 3 to 4 minutes until rhubarb is tender. Cool slightly. Place strawberries in a blender or food processor and process until smooth. Add cooled rhubarb and remaining ingredients. Process until smooth. Cover and refrigerate until ready to freeze. Pour into the ice cream maker and follow the manufacturer's instructions for freezing.

FROZEN STRAWBERRY YOGURT I

The natural fruit syrups make a flavorful quick yogurt or ice cream. Drain the yogurt a few hours before making this dessert, or the night before (see page 8).

1 cup drained yogurt
⅔ cup strawberry syrup
½ cup nonfat dry milk
1 pkg. (16 oz.) frozen unsweetened
    strawberries, partially defrosted

Place yogurt, syrup and dry milk in a blender or food processor and blend to combine. Add strawberries and process until smooth. Cover and chill until ready to freeze. Pour into the ice cream maker and follow the manufacturer's instructions for freezing.

FROZEN STRAWBERRY YOGURT II

Use fresh or unsweetened frozen strawberries to make this low calorie dessert. Remember to drain the yogurt a few hours before making this dessert, or the night before (see page 8).

1 cup drained yogurt
2½-3 cups fresh sliced strawberries,
   or 1 pkg. (16 oz.) frozen strawberries,
   partially defrosted
½ cup skim milk
1 tsp. unflavored gelatin, softened in 1 tbs. cold water
1 tbs. nonfat dry milk
2 tbs. NutraSweet sweetener

Combine yogurt and strawberries in a blender or food processor and blend for a few seconds to combine. Heat milk in a small saucepan. Add softened gelatin and stir to dissolve. Add milk, dry milk and NutraSweet to blender. Process until smooth and creamy. Cover and chill until ready to freeze. Pour into the ice cream maker and follow the manufacturer's instructions for freezing.

APRICOT ORANGE YOGURT

Makes: about 1 quart

Start by making 1 cup drained yogurt the night before (see page 8). This dessert has a wonderful creamy texture and bright apricot taste.

1 can (11 oz.) apricot nectar
1 cup orange juice
1 cup drained yogurt
¼ cup sugar
⅓ cup nonfat dry milk

Combine ingredients in a blender or food processor. Blend until smooth. Cover and chill in the refrigerator until ready to freeze. Blend for a few seconds before pouring into the ice cream maker. Follow the manufacturer's instructions for freezing.

DRIED PEACH SORBET

Many fruits are dried for the consumer today, and dried peaches are particularly flavorful. Try this refreshing low calorie, icy peach dessert.

10 oz. dried peaches (about 2 cups)
2½ cups water
1 tbs. lemon juice
1 tsp. vanilla extract
⅔ cup superfine sugar
grated nutmeg

Place peaches and water in a saucepan. Bring to a boil and simmer over low heat, covered, for about 15 minutes until peaches soften. Pour peach mixture into a blender or food processor. Add remaining ingredients and process until smooth. Chill in the refrigerator before freezing. Pour into the ice cream maker and follow the manufacturer's instructions for freezing.

DRIED APRICOT FROZEN YOGURT

Dried apricots are available year-round and make a great tangy, fruit-flavored dessert.

¾ cup dried apricots (about 5 oz.)
½ cup water
½ cup light corn syrup
2 tbs. lemon juice
½ cup nonfat dry milk
1 cup low fat milk
¼ tsp. almond extract
1 cup nonfat yogurt

Combine apricots and water in a small saucepan. Bring liquid to a boil, cover and simmer for about 15 minutes, until apricots are soft. Remove from heat; allow to cool to room temperature. Pour apricots and liquid into a blender or food processor and process until smooth. Add corn syrup, lemon juice, milks and almond extract. Process until well combined. Stir in yogurt and chill in the refrigerator until ready to freeze. Pour into the ice cream maker and follow the manufacturer's instructions for freezing.

KIWI ORANGE SHERBET

The small, brown kiwi has a wide distribution now that it is grown in the United States. Kiwis feel fairly firm even when quite ripe and have a delicious tart flavor.

3 kiwis
½ tsp. grated orange peel
½ cup orange juice
1¾ cups milk
3 tbs. nonfat dry milk
⅔ cup light corn syrup
1-2 drops green food coloring, optional

Cut out the small, hard cores on the stem end of the kiwis and discard. Peel and cut each kiwi into 8 pieces. Place kiwis, orange peel and juice in a blender or food processor and process until smooth. Add remaining ingredients and process until well combined. Cover and chill in the refrigerator until ready to freeze. Follow the manufacturer's instructions for freezing.

APPLE CINNAMON SHERBET

The creamy texture and slightly spicy flavors make this a fabulous finale for a fall or holiday dinner.

1¼ cups milk
½ cup superfine sugar
½ cup nonfat dry milk
2 tbs. lemon juice
2 cups canned smooth applesauce
¼ tsp. cinnamon
1 tsp. vanilla extract
pinch each ground nutmeg,
   ground cloves and salt

Pour milk, sugar, dry milk and lemon juice into a blender or food processor. Process on HIGH until well mixed. Add remaining ingredients and blend for another 30 seconds. Chill mixture in the refrigerator until ready to freeze. Pour mixture into the ice cream maker and follow the manufacturer's instructions for freezing.

MANGO ORANGE SHERBET

This is a delicious fruit dessert when you can get ripe mangoes. Mangoes have long fibers, so straining the fruit mixture makes a smoother sherbet.

½ cup sugar
½ cup water
2 large mangoes
1 tbs. lemon juice

½ cup frozen orange juice concentrate
1 cup whole milk
¼ cup nonfat dry milk
dash salt

Combine sugar and water in a small saucepan. Bring to a boil, reduce heat and simmer for about 5 minutes. Remove from heat and allow to cool to room temperature. Wash mangoes, cut in half and, while holding fruit over a bowl, twist to separate halves. Cut all mango pulp from seeds and scoop out from skins with a spoon. You should have about 1 cup fruit and juice. Place mango, lemon juice and orange juice concentrate in a blender or food processor. Process on HIGH for 15 to 20 seconds, scrape down sides of bowl and process until smooth, about 45 seconds. Add cooled sugar-water and remaining ingredients; process for another 10 to 15 seconds. Pour mango mixture through a strainer into a bowl or freezer container; place in the refrigerator to chill until ready to freeze. Pour into the ice cream maker and follow the manufacturer's instructions for freezing.

MELON YOGURT

Use either a ripe honeydew or cantaloupe melon for this refreshing dessert. Use Midori, which is a Japanese liqueur that has the flavor of a honeydew melon, with a fresh honeydew melon. Start draining the yogurt the night before (see page 8).

1½ cups pureed melon pieces (about 2 lb.)
1 cup drained yogurt
⅔ cup light corn syrup
2 tbs. nonfat dry milk
1 cup half-and-half
1 tsp. vanilla extract
2 tbs. Midori, optional

Combine ingredients in a blender or food processor and process until well combined. Cover and refrigerate until ready to freeze. Pour into the ice cream maker and follow the manufacturer's instructions for freezing.

GAZPACHO ICE

Makes: about 1 quart

Serve this in small goblets. As soon as ice is frozen, form or scoop into balls, place on a cold plate and put in the freezer until ready to serve. Leftovers can be softened in the microwave on DEFROST for 1 to 2 minutes, or put in the food processor to break up the ice crystals.

2 cups spicy tomato juice
1 large peeled seeded chopped fresh
   ripe tomato
1 cup peeled seeded chopped cucumber
¼ cup finely minced red onion
¼ cup finely minced peeled green or
   red pepper

4 oz. Egg Beaters, or egg substitute
2 tbs. sugar
2 tbs. full-flavored olive oil
2 tbs. red wine vinegar
salt and freshly ground pepper

Combine ingredients in a food processor or blender and pulse 5 or 6 times to combine ingredients but obtain a coarse texture. Cover and chill until ready to freeze. Pour into the ice cream maker and follow the manufacturer's instructions for freezing.

DELICIOUSLY LOW FAT 85

SAVORY CARROT FREEZE

Serve small scoops of this vibrant orange ice as a refreshing appetizer on a hot summer evening (or float a scoop in a bowl of chilled vichyssoise). This recipe can be doubled if you are serving more than 4 or 5 plates.

½ lb. carrots, peeled and thinly sliced
1 can (14½ oz.) chicken broth
1 tbs. chopped onion
2 quarter-sized pieces ginger root,
  peeled and chopped

1 tbs. balsamic vinegar
2 tbs. frozen orange juice concentrate,
  partially defrosted
salt to taste
generous amount white pepper

Combine carrots, chicken broth, onion and ginger in a small saucepan. Bring to a boil, lower heat, cover and cook for about 20 minutes until carrots and onion are very soft. Remove from heat and allow to cool to room temperature. Place carrots in a blender or food processor and add remaining ingredients. Blend until smooth. Adjust seasoning as needed. Cover and chill until ready to freeze. Pour into the ice cream maker and follow the manufacturer's instructions for freezing. Place in the freezer a few minutes after freezing to set up for easier serving. Scoop out small portions just before serving.

PINEAPPLE SHERBET

Makes: about 1 quart

This is a year-round favorite. All you need is a couple of cans of crushed pineapple on the pantry shelf. This makes a great ice cream pie with a chocolate crust.

2 cans (8 oz. each) crushed unsweetened
  pineapple with juice
2/3 cup light corn syrup
1½ cups milk
2 tbs. Triple Sec, or orange juice

Pour pineapple with juice and remaining ingredients in a blender or food processor. Process until smooth. Chill in the refrigerator until ready to freeze. Pour mixture through a strainer into the ice cream maker. Follow the manufacturer's instructions for freezing.

DELICIOUSLY LOW FAT 87

PIÑA COLADA SHERBET

Frozen piña colada mix makes a quick base for a delicious sherbet.

1 can (10 oz.) piña colada mix, partially defrosted
2½ cups milk
2 tbs. nonfat dry milk
2 tbs. dark rum
dash salt

Combine ingredients in a blender or food processor and process until dry milk is dissolved. Cover and chill in the refrigerator until ready to freeze. Pour into the ice cream maker and follow the manufacturer's instructions for freezing.

PINEAPPLE COCONUT SHERBET

Pineapple and coconut are complementary flavors that make a great ending for a summer dinner or are delicious after slightly spicy food.

2 cans (11.5 oz. each) pineapple coconut nectar
4 oz. Egg Beaters, or egg substitute
¼ cup corn syrup
⅓ cup nonfat dry milk
2 tbs. lemon juice
dash salt

Combine ingredients in a blender or food processor and blend until smooth. Cover and refrigerate until ready to freeze. Pour into the ice cream maker and follow the manufacturer's instructions for freezing.

BANANA DAIQUIRI SHERBET

Tropical flavors of banana, lime and rum make an easy summer dessert. The riper the bananas, the better. Coarsely chopped macadamia nuts sprinkled over each serving add a nice touch.

2 cups milk
1 cup mashed ripe bananas (about 2 large)
$\frac{1}{2}$ cup corn syrup
$\frac{1}{3}$ cup nonfat dry milk
$\frac{1}{2}$ tsp. grated lime peel
$\frac{1}{4}$ cup lime juice
2 tbs. dark rum
dash salt

Combine ingredients in a blender or food processor and blend until smooth. Cover and chill in the refrigerator until ready to freeze. Blend for a few seconds before pouring into the ice cream maker. Follow the manufacturer's instructions for freezing.

BITTERSWEET CHOCOLATE MOCHA SORBET

This is marvelous on its own or paired with a scoop of vanilla or butterscotch ice cream.

6 oz. bittersweet chocolate, melted
1 tbs. vegetable oil
2½ cups water
¼ cup sugar

2 tbs. instant espresso coffee powder
½ cup light corn syrup
1 tsp. vanilla extract
dash salt

Melt chocolate in a microwave on MEDIUM or in the top of a double boiler. Stir in oil when chocolate is completely melted and smooth. In a small saucepan, bring water and sugar to a boil and cook for 2 to 3 minutes to dissolve sugar. Stir in coffee. Combine warm melted chocolate with hot water mixture and mix well. Pour into a blender; add corn syrup, vanilla and salt. Blend well. Chill in the refrigerator until ready to freeze. Blend for a few seconds before pouring into the ice cream maker. Follow the manufacturer's instructions for freezing.

SUGAR-FREE CAPPUCCINO ICE CREAM

This is delicious even if you know it is sugar-free.

1 tsp. plain gelatin
1½ cups low fat milk
2 tbs. instant espresso coffee powder
3½ tsp. NutraSweet sweetener
2 tbs. nonfat dry milk
1½ cups buttermilk
1 tsp. vanilla extract
¼ tsp. cinnamon
dash salt

Soften gelatin in ½ cup milk. Heat in a small saucepan and add coffee. Cook over low heat until gelatin and coffee dissolve. Remove from heat, stir in NutraSweet, and place saucepan in another bowl of cold or ice water to cool to room temperature. Pour mixture into a blender or food processor, add rest of milk and remaining ingredients and blend until smooth. Cover and chill in the refrigerator until ready to freeze. Blend for a few seconds before pouring into the ice cream maker. Follow the manufacturer's instructions for freezing.

SUGAR-FREE CHOCOLATE ICE CREAM

Makes: about 1 quart

This is a sweet treat for those watching calories and sugar intake.

1 tsp. plain gelatin
2½ cups low fat milk
½ cup Nestlé Quik Sugar Free chocolate drink mix
1 cup drained yogurt (see page 8)
1 tsp. vanilla extract
dash salt

Soften gelatin in ½ cup milk. Heat in a small saucepan until gelatin dissolves. Remove from heat and place saucepan in another bowl of cold or ice water to cool mixture to room temperature. Pour mixture into a blender or food processor. Add remaining milk, Quik, yogurt, vanilla and salt. Blend until smooth. Cover and chill in the refrigerator until ready to freeze. Blend for a few seconds before pouring into the ice cream maker. Follow the manufacturer's instructions for freezing.

CHOCOLATE BUTTERMILK ICE CREAM

Here is a tangy, low calorie chocolate ice cream.

1½ cups milk
⅓ cup unsweetened cocoa
½ cup sugar
1 tsp. instant espresso coffee powder
2 cups buttermilk
3 tbs. nonfat dry milk
2 tsp. vanilla extract
dash salt

Combine ½ cup milk, cocoa, sugar and coffee in a small saucepan. Heat until sugar melts and ingredients are well combined. Remove from heat and place saucepan in another bowl of cold or ice water to cool to room temperature. Pour mixture into a blender or food processor and add remaining ingredients. Process until smooth. Cover and chill in the refrigerator until ready to freeze. Blend for a few seconds before pouring into the ice cream maker. Follow the manufacturer's instructions for freezing.

EASY CHOCOLATE FROZEN YOGURT

Makes: about 1 quart

All you need is some prepared vanilla yogurt and chocolate-flavored syrup to make a quick dessert treat.

3 cartons (8 oz. each) low fat vanilla yogurt
¾ cup milk
½ cup chocolate-flavored syrup
1 tbs. dark rum, optional
dash salt

Pour all ingredients into a blender or food processor. Process on HIGH until well combined, about 30 to 45 seconds. Pour into the ice cream maker and follow the manufacturer's instructions for freezing.

ESPRESSO SHERBET

This deep coffee-flavored sherbet makes a wonderful dessert for a rich dinner.

3 cups milk
2 tbs. instant espresso coffee powder
1 tbs. unsweetened cocoa
½ cup nonfat dry milk
⅔ cup dark corn syrup
2 tsp. vanilla extract
pinch grated nutmeg
dash salt

Combine ½ cup milk, coffee and cocoa in a small saucepan. Heat until coffee and cocoa have dissolved. Cool slightly. Combine coffee mixture with remaining ingredients in a blender or food processor. Process until smooth. Cover and refrigerate until ready to freeze. Pour into the ice cream maker and follow the manufacturer's instructions for freezing.

MAPLE PECAN ICE CREAM

Toasted pecans accent the delicious maple syrup flavor in this ice cream.

$\frac{1}{2}$ cup chopped toasted pecans
4 oz. Egg Beaters, or egg substitute
$\frac{3}{4}$ cup maple syrup
2 cups buttermilk
1 cup milk
2 tbs. nonfat dry milk
2 tsp. vanilla extract
dash salt

Lightly toast pecans in a 350° oven and set aside to cool. Combine all ingredients except pecans in a blender or food processor. Process until well combined. Cover and refrigerate until ready to freeze. Blend for a few seconds before pouring into the ice cream maker. Follow the manufacturer's instructions for freezing. About a minute before ice cream is frozen, add nuts.

FAT-FREE

NO FAT, NO SALT VANILLA ICE CREAM

Makes: about 1 quart

Here is an ice cream for dessert lovers who are minding their cholesterol. Serve with fresh sliced strawberries, peaches or a few raspberries.

4 oz. Egg Beaters, or egg substitute
1 cup nonfat sour cream
¼ cup nonfat dry milk
2 cups skim milk
⅔ cup sugar
1 tbs. vanilla extract
¼ tsp. lemon or almond extract

Combine ingredients in a blender or food processor and process until sugar and milk have dissolved and mixture is smooth. Chill in the refrigerator until ready to freeze. Pour into the ice cream maker and follow the manufacturer's instructions for freezing.

NO FAT, NO SALT, NO SUGAR VANILLA ICE CREAM

This tasty ice cream uses a sugar substitute instead of sugar.

1 tsp. unflavored gelatin
2¼ cups cold skim milk
1 cup nonfat dry milk
4 oz. Egg Beaters, or egg substitute

5 tsp. NutraSweet sweetener
⅛ tsp. lemon or almond extract
2 tsp. vanilla extract

Sprinkle gelatin over skim milk in a small saucepan and allow gelatin to soften for a few minutes. Stir mixture over low heat until gelatin completely dissolves. Remove from heat and place saucepan in another bowl of cold or ice water to cool to room temperature. Combine remaining ingredients in a blender or food processor and process until well combined. Add milk-gelatin mixture and blend for a few more seconds. Chill in the refrigerator until ready to freeze. Blend for a few seconds before pouring mixture through a strainer into the ice cream maker. Follow the manufacturer's instructions for freezing.

APPLE JUICE SORBET

This nonfat, easy sorbet starts with frozen apple juice concentrate.

1 can (12 oz.) frozen apple juice concentrate, partially defrosted
2 cups water
2 tbs. lemon juice
⅓ cup light corn syrup

   Place ingredients in a blender or food processor and process until smooth. Chill in the refrigerator until ready to freeze. Pour into the ice cream maker and follow the manufacturer's instructions for freezing.

PINK GRAPEFRUIT SORBET

This is a refreshingly tart, year-round dessert. If you use regular frozen grapefruit juice concentrate, increase the corn syrup to ¾ cup.

1 can (6 oz.) frozen pink grapefruit juice
  concentrate, partially defrosted
2¼ cups water
½ cup corn syrup

Combine ingredients in a blender or food processor. Blend until smooth. Cover and refrigerate until ready to freeze. Pour into the ice cream maker and follow the manufacturer's instructions for freezing.

WATERMELON SORBET

This refreshing sorbet is a pretty pink color and really tastes like watermelon. It does take a little time to remove the seeds.

4½-5 lb. piece watermelon
½ cup sugar
⅔ cup water

4 oz. Egg Beaters, or egg substitute
2 tbs. lemon juice
dash salt

Remove watermelon pulp from rind and scrape out seeds, saving as much juice as possible. Cut watermelon into small chunks and place in a blender or food processor. Process until smooth. Strain through a coarse sieve to remove any small white seeds. There should be approximately 3 cups melon juice. Return melon juice to blender. Combine sugar and water in a small saucepan. Bring to a boil and cook for 3 to 4 minutes until sugar is completely dissolved. Remove from heat and place saucepan in another bowl of cold or ice water to cool mixture. Add to melon juice along with remaining ingredients. Process until smooth. Cover and chill in the refrigerator until ready to freeze. Blend for a few seconds before pouring into the ice cream maker. Follow the manufacturer's instructions for freezing.

BLOOD ORANGE SORBET

The gorgeous, red-juiced blood oranges make a beautiful and delicious sorbet.

1 orange peel for garnish
3 cups blood orange juice
1 cup sugar
4 oz. Egg Beaters, or egg substitute
2 tbs. Triple Sec, or orange liqueur, optional

Finely grate and reserve 1 orange peel for garnish. Combine remaining ingredients in a blender or food processor and process until well combined. Cover and refrigerate until ready to freeze. Pour mixture into the ice cream maker and follow the manufacturer's instructions for freezing. Garnish individual servings of sorbet with a little orange peel.

CRANBERRY ORANGE SORBET

This makes an attractive, delicious and low calorie finale for an autumn or holiday dinner. Serve alone or with some thin, crisp cookies.

8 oz. fresh cranberries, washed
  and stemmed
1 cup sugar
2 cups water
2 tbs. frozen orange juice concentrate
1 pkg. unflavored gelatin, dissolved
  in ¼ cup cold water

Combine cranberries, sugar, water and orange Juice in a medium saucepan. Bring liquid to a boil and simmer for about 10 minutes until cranberries soften and split open. Remove from heat and stir in dissolved gelatin. Allow to cool to room temperature. Pour into a blender or food processor and process until smooth. Chill in the refrigerator until ready to freeze. Pour through a strainer into the ice cream maker and follow the manufacturer's instructions for freezing.

DRIED PEAR SORBET

Sorbets satisfy the sweet tooth without adding fat or many calories. Dried fruits make a perfect base for intensely flavored sorbets and ices.

$\frac{1}{2}$ cup water
$\frac{1}{2}$ cup sugar
8 oz. dried pears (about $1\frac{1}{2}$ cups)
2 cups water
$\frac{1}{4}$ cup lime juice
dash salt

Combine $\frac{1}{2}$ cup water with sugar in a small saucepan. Bring to a boil and simmer for 5 minutes to make a simple syrup. Combine dried pears and 2 cups water in a saucepan and bring to a boil. Reduce heat, cover and simmer for 15 minutes until pears soften. Allow to cool slightly and pour into a blender or food processor with simple syrup mixture and remaining ingredients. Process until smooth. Chill in the refrigerator before freezing. Blend mixture for a few seconds before pouring through a strainer into the ice cream maker. Follow the manufacturer's instructions for freezing.

FRESH PLUM SORBET

Ripe, juicy plums make a light and pretty dessert sorbet.

1¼ cups sugar
1 cup water
1-inch piece cinnamon stick
3½-4 cups halved pitted red plums
2 tbs. lemon juice
½ tsp. vanilla extract
dash salt

In a 2- to 3-quart saucepan, combine sugar, water and cinnamon stick. Bring to a boil over high heat, stirring until sugar dissolves. Add plums; continue boiling, uncovered, for 2 minutes. Cover, reduce heat and simmer for 8 to 10 minutes or until plums are very tender. Remove plums from heat and discard cinnamon stick. Cool slightly and pour plum mixture into a food processor or blender and process until smooth. Stir in lemon juice, vanilla and salt. Cover and refrigerate until thoroughly chilled. Pour into the ice cream maker and follow the manufacturer's instructions for freezing.

MARGARITA SORBET

Makes: about 1 quart

This is an easy, not-too-sweet summer treat. It melts fast, so serve it with straws and a spoon for an afternoon party or Mexican-style brunch.

1 can (10 oz.) frozen margarita mix,
   partially defrosted
2¼ cups water
¼ cup tequila
dash salt

Combine ingredients in a blender and process until smooth. Pour into an ice cream maker and follow the manufacturer's instructions for freezing.

VARIATION

Add fresh sliced peaches, strawberries or kiwis and a tablespoon or two of superfine sugar to the blender mix.

STRAWBERRY GUAVA NECTAR SHERBET Makes: about 1 quart

The fresh fruit flavors of strawberry and guava make a nonfat, low sodium and totally delicious sherbet.

2 cans (11½ oz. each) strawberry guava nectar
½ cup nonfat dry milk
2 tbs. lemon juice
¼ cup sugar
dash salt
fresh strawberry slices for garnish

Place all ingredients except strawberry slices in a blender. Process on HIGH until smooth. Chill in the refrigerator until ready to freeze. Pour into the ice cream maker and follow the manufacturer's instructions for freezing. Garnish with a few fresh strawberry slices or serve with *Lemon Almond Biscotti*, page 124.

ORANGE SPICED TEA SHERBET

Constant Comment tea flavors this low calorie dessert.

3 cups milk
½ cup sugar
4 Constant Comment tea bags
¼ cup nonfat dry milk
4 oz. Egg Beaters, or egg substitute
dash salt

Combine 1 cup milk and sugar in a small saucepan. Bring almost to a boil, add tea bags, cover and steep for about 20 minutes. Pour mixture through a strainer into a blender or food processor, pressing out as much liquid from the tea bags as possible. Add remaining ingredients and process until smooth. Cover and chill in the refrigerator until ready to freeze. Pour into the ice cream maker and follow the manufacturer's instructions for freezing.

RHUBARB SHERBET

Makes: about 1 quart

This lovely pink, slightly tart sherbet makes a refreshing springtime dessert. Sliced or pureed fresh strawberries are a delicious accompaniment.

¾ cup water
¾ cup sugar
1 lb. rhubarb, cut into 1-inch pieces
⅔ cup nonfat dry milk
⅔ cup orange juice
2 tbs. Triple Sec, or orange-flavored liqueur
dash salt

Bring water and sugar to a boil in a medium saucepan, lower heat and simmer for 3 to 4 minutes until sugar is dissolved. Add rhubarb pieces, cover and cook over low heat for about 5 minutes, until rhubarb is soft. Remove from heat, uncover and allow to cool to room temperature. Pour rhubarb into a blender or food processor, add remaining ingredients and process until smooth. Chill in the refrigerator until ready to freeze. Pour into the ice cream maker and follow the manufacturer's instructions for freezing.

RED WINE PEAR ICE

Makes: about 3 cups

This rosy, pear-flavored ice with just a hint of cinnamon is a delicious finale for an autumn or holiday dinner.

8 oz. dried pears
2 cups dry red wine
$^2/_3$ cup light corn syrup
2 tbs. lemon juice
$^1/_8$ tsp. cinnamon
pinch ground ginger
dash salt

Place pears and wine in a saucepan. Bring wine to a boil, lower heat and simmer covered for about 15 minutes until pears soften. Remove from heat; add corn syrup, stirring to dissolve. Cool slightly and pour pear mixture into a blender or food processor. Process until smooth. Add remaining ingredients. Chill in the refrigerator before freezing. Pour mixture into the ice cream maker and follow the manufacturer's instructions for freezing.

STRAWBERRY DAIQUIRI ICE

The frozen drink mixes make a terrific base for frozen desserts.

⅔ cup frozen strawberry daiquiri mix,
  defrosted but undiluted
1¾ cups water
¼ cup light rum, or orange juice
1 pkg. (16 oz.) frozen strawberries, defrosted,
  or 2 cups fresh sliced strawberries

Place all ingredients in a blender or food processor and blend until smooth. Cover and chill until ready to freeze. Pour into the ice cream maker and follow the manufacturer's instructions for freezing.

SAUCES

Some people like their ice cream plain, but it is always tempting to embellish a good thing with a creamy sauce or a fresh fruit garnish. Ice cream is a perfect foil for your favorite gooey concoction. Sauces can be hot, cold or in between.

Try topping a wonderful homemade vanilla ice cream with a hot caramel sauce, or try a bittersweet chocolate sauce over a lighter chocolate ice cream.

Make some fresh fruit sauces when peaches, strawberries, raspberries and blueberries are in season. The ripe, sweet fruit adds a delicious accent. Try pairing a fresh peach sauce with vanilla ice cream and fresh raspberries, or make a raspberry sauce to serve with fresh peach ice cream. Lemon ice cream and blueberries make a wonderful combination. Vanilla ice cream with a fresh strawberry sauce and ripe raspberries is a classic treat.

BUTTERSCOTCH SAUCE

This is a delicious sundae topping. Add a sprinkle of nuts, too, if the occasion demands.

1/2 cup dark corn syrup
1/4 cup brown sugar
1/4 cup sugar
1/4 cup half-and-half
1 tbs. butter
dash salt
1 tsp. vanilla extract

Combine ingredients except vanilla in a small saucepan. Bring mixture to a full boil. Cook for 5 minutes. Remove from heat and add vanilla. Serve warm.

CARAMEL SAUCE

This is a traditional caramel sauce that can be made ahead and reheated in the microwave just before serving.

1 cup sugar
1 cup half-and-half
1 tbs. butter
dash salt
¼ tsp. vanilla extract

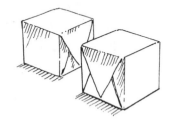

Place sugar in a heavy 10-inch skillet. Stir with a fork over low heat until sugar melts and turns a golden brown. Remove from heat and slowly pour half-and-half down side of skillet, being careful to keep your hand away from the steam. Sugar will form a big ball. Free sugar from bottom of skillet with fork and return to heat. Stir to dissolve. When sauce is smooth, remove from heat and stir in butter and salt. Allow to cool slightly and stir in vanilla. Serve hot over your favorite ice cream.

QUICK CARAMEL SAUCE

Makes: 1¼ cups

This is an easy and delicious ice cream sauce. You can also use some of it to make ***Easy Caramel Ice Cream****, page 19. Reheat in the microwave.*

½ lb. caramels
½ cup milk

Place caramels and milk in a heavy saucepan. Stir slowly over low heat until caramels melt and make a smooth sauce. Serve warm.

RASPBERRY SAUCE

Makes: about ⅔ cup

A package of frozen raspberries makes a gorgeous full-flavored ice cream sauce, or turn it into ***Raspberry Sherbet****, page 70.*

1 pkg. (10 oz.) frozen raspberries,
  defrosted
2 tbs. sugar

1 tbs. Triple Sec, or 2 tbs.
  orange juice

Combine ingredients in a blender or food processor and process until smooth. Pour through a strainer, pressing out as much fruit and liquid as possible. Discard seeds. Refrigerate until ready to serve.

APRICOT SAUCE

*This simple sauce complements a variety of ice creams. Make an apricot sundae with vanilla ice cream and **Apricot Orange Yogurt**, page 78. Sprinkle with a few toasted almonds and maybe some whipped cream.*

½ cup apricot jam
½ cup canned apricot nectar
1 tbs. brandy, or orange-flavored liqueur

Combine jam and nectar in a small saucepan. Bring to a boil, lower heat and cook for 5 to 6 minutes, until jam dissolves. Remove from heat, add brandy and cool to room temperature, or refrigerate until ready to serve.

BLUEBERRY SAUCE

This is a wonderful sauce on lemon, orange or strawberry ice cream. The berries add a nice texture. Double the sauce if you need more servings.

½ cup water
⅓ cup sugar
2 tbs. lemon juice
1 tsp. cornstarch
1 tbs. Triple Sec, or orange-flavored liqueur
1 cup blueberries, washed and stemmed

Combine ½ cup water and sugar in a small saucepan. Bring to a boil to dissolve sugar. Add lemon juice. Dissolve cornstarch in Triple Sec. Add to water-sugar mixture and cook over low heat for 1 to 2 minutes until sauce thickens slightly and turns clear. Stir blueberries into sauce and heat through. Serve warm or chilled.

MEXICAN CHOCOLATE SAUCE

Makes: ¾ cup

This cinnamon-orange chocolate sauce can be served hot or cold over ice cream.

1 round (3.1 oz.) Ibarra chocolate,
  broken into pieces

½ cup heavy cream
1 tbs. brandy, or dark rum

Heat chocolate and cream together over low heat until chocolate melts and mixture is smooth and creamy. Stir in brandy. Refrigerate if not serving immediately.

ZINFANDEL SAUCE

Makes: about 1½ cups

This sauce is particularly delicious over **Frozen Zabaglione***, page 35.*

1½ cups red zinfandel wine, or fruity
  young red wine
½ cup sugar
½ grated orange peel

2 tbs. orange juice
½ stick cinnamon
3 whole cloves

Combine ingredients in a small saucepan. Bring to a boil and simmer for about 5 minutes. Strain into a small bowl, cool to room temperature, cover and refrigerate until ready to use.

ICE CREAM ACCOMPANIMENTS

Ice cream and cookies are a classic combination. A cookie or two will provide a nice crunchy counterpoint to cold, creamy ice cream or add a contrasting flavor to a simple sherbet or ice. Cookie cups make an elegant edible dish for ice cream, or you can melt chocolate in foil cupcake papers to form little cups. Cookies make great ice cream sandwiches, too.

CHOCOLATE BISCOTTI

Whole hazelnuts, walnuts, almonds or pecans are all delicious in this Italian-style cookie.

½ cup unsalted butter, melted
1 cup sugar
1 tsp. vanilla extract
1 tsp. chocolate extract
3 tbs. dark rum, or Frangelico
3 eggs
2½ cups all-purpose flour
3 tbs. unsweetened cocoa
1½ tsp. baking powder
1 cup whole hazelnuts, toasted

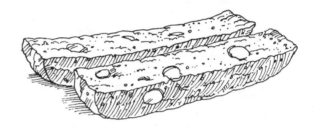

Preheat the oven to 350°. Mix butter, sugar, vanilla, chocolate extract and rum in a bowl. Whisk eggs and stir into butter-sugar mixture. Sift flour, cocoa and baking powder together and add to bowl, stirring well to combine. Stir in nuts. Form into 2 loaves about 3 inches wide and ¾-inch high on a well-greased or parchment-paper-lined cookie sheet. Bake for 20 to 25 minutes until slightly firm to the touch. Top of loaves may crack. Remove from oven and allow to cool for 5 to 10 minutes. Reduce oven to 300°. Cut loaves into ½-inch slices and place on cookie sheet. Return to oven for about 20 minutes to crisp. Turn cookies over and crisp other side for an additional 15 to 20 minutes. Remove from oven and allow to cool. Store in an airtight container.

NOTE: To toast hazelnuts, put them in a shallow saucepan in a preheated 350° oven. Shake saucepan frequently to rotate nuts. When nuts start to brown and begin to smell toasty, remove from oven and turn into a rough terry towel. Rub nuts in towel to loosen brown skin. Remove as much of skin as possible. Cool before adding to cookie dough.

LEMON ALMOND BISCOTTI

Try these with chocolate ice cream or fruit-flavored sherbets.

$\frac{1}{2}$ cup unsalted butter, melted
$1\frac{1}{4}$ cups sugar
1 tsp. vanilla extract
$1\frac{1}{2}$ tsp. lemon extract
1 grated lemon peel

3 tbs. lemon juice
3 eggs
$2\frac{1}{2}$ cups all-purpose flour
1 tsp. baking soda
1 cup toasted slivered almonds

Preheat the oven to 350°. Combine butter, sugar, vanilla, lemon extract, peel and juice in a mixing bowl. Whisk eggs together and add to butter-sugar mixture. Sift flour and soda together and add to mixing bowl. Stir well to combine. Add almonds. Form into 2 loaves about 3 inches wide and $\frac{3}{4}$-inch high on a well-greased or parchment-paper-lined cookie sheet. Bake for 20 to 25 minutes until slightly firm to the touch. Tops of loaves may crack. Remove from oven and allow to cool for 5 to 10 minutes. Reduce oven to 300°. Cut loaves into $\frac{1}{2}$-inch slices and place on cookie sheet. Return to oven for about 20 minutes to crisp. Turn cookies over and crisp other side for an additional 15 to 20 minutes. Remove from oven and allow to cool. Store in an airtight container.

LACE COOKIES

These crisp, elegant cookies make delicious cookie cups, or you can roll them into cylinders or cone shapes. It is easier to shape them while warm.

¼ cup light corn syrup
3 tbs. butter
⅓ cup brown sugar
½ cup sifted cake flour

½ cup toasted finely chopped or
   ground almonds, pecans or walnuts
pinch salt

Preheat the oven to 325°. Prepare the cookie sheets by oiling or lining with parchment paper. Combine syrup, butter and brown sugar in a small saucepan. Bring to a boil and remove from heat. Stir in flour, nuts and salt. Drop heaping teaspoonfuls of batter onto prepared cookie sheets about 4 inches apart. Bake for 9 to 11 minutes until golden brown. Cool for 1 to 2 minutes and remove from cookie sheets with a wide spatula. Roll into cone shapes or place warm cookies over oiled custard cups or glasses to make cookie cups. Drape cookies over a rolling pin to make cookie tiles. If they are difficult to form, return to oven for a few minutes until they soften. Store these in an airtight container as soon as they have cooled to keep them from absorbing moisture from the air.

COOKIE CUPS

If you are looking for an elegant, easy dessert, serve any wonderful homemade ice cream in these delicate cookie cups. These can be made ahead and kept in an airtight container for a day or two before serving.

¼ cup butter, room temperature
⅓ cup sugar
¼ cup Egg Beaters, or egg whites
½ tsp. grated lemon peel
½ tsp. vanilla extract
⅓ cup sifted all-purpose flour
pinch salt

Preheat the oven to 400°. Line 2 cookie sheets with parchment paper or foil. Using a 5-inch diameter bowl, trace 2 circles on each sheet. Oil the backs of 2 baking cups or small bowls to be used for forming the cookie cups. Cream butter and sugar together until light and fluffy. Beat in Egg Beaters. Add lemon peel and vanilla. Fold sifted flour and salt into mixture. Using 1 heaping tablespoon cookie dough for each cookie cup, place dough in center of marked circles on cookie sheets and spread evenly about ⅛-inch thick over entire circle. Bake 1 cookie sheet of 2 circles at a time for easier handling. Bake cookies for about 4 to 5 minutes until edges are lightly browned. Remove from oven and slide a large spatula under cookie to lift from cookie sheet. Quickly drape hot cookie over oiled baking cup or bowl. Remove second cookie and form in same manner. If cookies do not seem soft and pliable, return cookie sheet to oven to heat slightly, and remove to form over cups. Continue to bake and mold remaining cookies. Allow to cool. Store in an airtight container until ready to use.

SERVING SUGGESTIONS

Place each cookie cup on a serving plate; fill with 1 or 2 scoops of ice cream and garnish with fresh fruit sauce, sprigs of mint, whipped cream or chocolate shavings.

CRISP GINGERSNAPS

This old-fashioned, gingery cookie is delicious served beside a dish of ice cream. Form slightly larger cookies to make ice cream sandwiches.

¾ cup shortening, or margarine
1 cup sugar, plus 2 tbs.
¼ cup dark molasses
1 egg, lightly beaten
2 cups all-purpose flour

2 tsp. baking soda
1 tsp. ground ginger
1 tsp. cinnamon
½ tsp. ground cloves
dash salt

Preheat the oven to 350°. Prepare the cookie sheets by oiling or lining with parchment paper. With a mixer, cream shortening and 1 cup sugar until light and fluffy. Add molasses and egg. Mix well. Sift flour, soda, spices and salt. Add to sugar mixture, beating until well combined. Form cookie dough into 1- or 1½-inch diameter balls. Place 2 tbs. sugar on a small plate. Roll cookie balls in sugar. Place on prepared cookie sheets about 2 inches apart. Bake for about 15 minutes until lightly browned. Remove to cooling rack.

OLD-FASHIONED
SODA FOUNTAIN TREATS

Ice cream specialty stores are noted for serving wonderful cold ice cream sundaes, sodas, floats and banana splits. These can be easily duplicated with delicious home-made ice cream and toppings from the supermarket, or your own sauces.

A make-your-own ice cream or dessert bar is fun for a small group after a barbecue or summer dinner. Depending on how much time you have, either make or buy the ice cream and toppings. Scoop out several different kinds of ice cream balls ahead of time and keep them in the freezer. Set up the serving area with different ice cream toppings, sauces, sliced fruit and nuts. Put out a plate of homemade cookies, too.

Unusual goblets, tall glasses, pretty glass dishes, long-handled spoons and straws add a festive air to the party.

Some soda fountain tips:

- If you are making a number of servings, make and scoop out the ice cream ahead of time. Place scoops of ice cream on a large, chilled plate and place it in the freezer until serving time.
- Dip the ice cream scoop in warm water between scoops to keep ice cream from sticking.
- Use a regular ice cream dipper for round balls or a spade-type server for oval shapes, or form scoops with a pair of large tablespoons.
- Chill club soda, root beer, fruit juice or other carbonated beverages to be used.
- Use chilled glasses, plates or dishes to avoid instant meltdown.
- Toast nuts for 5 to 10 minutes in a low temperature oven to bring out the flavors.
- Prepare syrups, toppings and nuts, and have whipped cream close at hand for assembling the ice cream creation.
- Fresh raspberries, blueberries, sliced strawberries, peaches or bananas make colorful and tasty accents.

The following recipes are suggested amounts for individual servings and can easily be doubled or tripled as required. Feel free to use your own favorite combinations. If you really love ice cream, increase the proportions accordingly.

ICE CREAM SUNDAES

Almost every child from the age of 5 knows how to put together a sundae with personal favorite flavors.

A scoop or two of ice cream receives a generous dollop of 2 to 3 tablespoons flavorful syrup, ice cream topping or sauce. Chopped nuts, whipped cream and maraschino cherries add the final touches.

One of the simplest sundaes is a scoop of ice cream topped with a splash of your favorite after-dinner liqueur.

To make a hot chocolate fudge sundae, heat the chocolate sauce before pouring it over the ice cream. Top with nuts and whipped cream.

The sky is the limit when it comes to creating out-of-this-world sundaes!

ICE CREAM DRINKS

Serve ice cream in the form of an after-dinner drink for an easy, elegant dessert. Many varieties of fruit, coffee, and other flavored liqueurs and brandies are available. Put together your favorite flavors and blend to a creamy finish.

In this chapter are a few classic combinations.

BANANA SPLIT

A banana split is total indulgence! Substitute marshmallow sauce for the crushed pineapple if you prefer.

1 banana
lemon juice, optional
1 scoop each chocolate, strawberry
  and vanilla ice cream
1-2 tbs. chocolate sauce
1-2 tbs. crushed strawberries,
  or strawberry sauce
1-2 tbs. crushed pineapple
finely chopped nuts
whipped cream
maraschino cherries

Split banana in half, lengthwise. Brush banana with lemon juice if not using immediately. Place banana halves in a shallow, long dish. Arrange scoops of ice cream on top of banana. Top chocolate ice cream with chocolate sauce, strawberry ice cream with strawberries and vanilla ice cream with pineapple. Sprinkle with nuts and dollops of whipped cream. Place maraschino cherries on last. Serve immediately.

DOUBLE CHOCOLATE MALTED MILK

Servings: 1

Here is a cold, creamy way to satisfy a sweet tooth.

1 cup cold milk
3 tbs. chocolate syrup
1 tbs. malted milk powder

2 large scoops chocolate ice cream
whipped cream for garnish, optional

Place ingredients in a blender and process on HIGH for 30 seconds or until smooth and creamy. Serve in a tall, chilled glass with a straw. Garnish with whipped cream, if desired.

MAPLE MALTED MILK

Servings: 1

Maple syrup makes a delicious malt.

1 cup cold milk
¼ cup maple syrup
1 tbs. malted milk powder

2 large scoops vanilla ice cream
whipped cream for garnish, optional

Place ingredients in a blender and process on HIGH for 30 seconds or until smooth and creamy. Serve in a tall, chilled glass with a straw. Garnish with whipped cream, if desired.

ROOT BEER FLOAT

This old-fashioned favorite is a summertime treat. If watching calories, use diet root beer and low fat ice cream.

chilled root beer
1 large scoop vanilla ice cream

Pour root beer gently down the side of a tall, chilled 12- to 16-ounce glass, allowing room for ice cream. Add ice cream on top; do not stir. Serve with a straw and a long-handled iced tea spoon.

BROWN COW

This ice cream float is made with a cola instead of root beer.

1/4 cup cold milk
1 tbs. chocolate syrup

chilled cola drink
1 large scoop vanilla ice cream

Combine milk and syrup in a tall, chilled 12- to 16-ounce glass. Stir to combine flavors. Add cola by pouring gently down side of glass to reduce foaming, leaving room for ice cream. Stir gently and add ice cream. Serve immediately with a straw and a long-handled iced tea spoon.

FRESH FRUIT MILK SHAKE

Strawberries, raspberries or peaches all make wonderful milk shakes. Use straw-berry or peach ice cream instead of vanilla.

½ cup fresh peeled sliced fruit
1 tbs. sugar
½ cup cold milk
2 scoops ice cream

Place all ingredients in a blender and process on HIGH until smooth and creamy. Serve in a tall, chilled glass with a straw.

BASIC MILK SHAKE

Use your favorite flavor combinations.

1 cup cold milk
3 tbs. flavored syrup
2 scoops ice cream

Place ingredients in a blender and process on HIGH for about 30 seconds until smooth and creamy. Serve in a tall, chilled glass with a straw.

COMBINATION SUGGESTIONS

- raspberry syrup with strawberry ice cream or yogurt
- butterscotch syrup with vanilla ice cream or *Butterscotch Ice Cream*, page 42
- chocolate syrup with *Mexican Chocolate Ice Cream*, page 28
- *Caramel Sauce*, page 116, with *Creamy Peanut Butter Ice Cream*, page 40

ICE CREAM SODA

The secret to a delicious soda is to serve it while it is still fizzing.

¼ cup cold milk
2 tbs. flavored syrup
2 scoops ice cream

cold club soda
whipped cream for garnish
maraschino cherry for garnish

Combine milk and flavored syrup and pour into a tall, chilled glass. Add 1 scoop ice cream with a little soda and, using a long-handled spoon, press ice cream into mixture. Add remaining ice cream and fill glass with club soda. Garnish with whipped cream and cherry. Serve immediately with a straw and a long-handled iced tea spoon.

COMBINATION SUGGESTIONS
- raspberry syrup with *Fresh Peach Ice Cream*, page 50
- chocolate syrup with *Coffee Ice Cream*, page 25
- cherry syrup with *Sweet Cherry Ice Cream*, page 33
- strawberry syrup with *Old-Fashioned Lemon Ice Cream*, page 34

PEACH MELBA SUNDAE

Peaches and raspberries are a classic combination.

½ peeled sliced fresh peach, or canned peach slices
1 scoop vanilla ice cream
2 tbs. *Raspberry Sauce*, page 117
fresh raspberries for garnish
whipped cream for garnish
sliced almonds for garnish, optional

Place peaches in a small dessert dish, top with ice cream and add *Raspberry Sauce*. Garnish with fresh raspberries, a dollop of whipped cream and some sliced almonds, if desired.

KIR ROYALE

This is an elegant little dessert. Use a sweet champagne.

1 scoop raspberry sherbet
1 tsp. crème de cassis
⅓ cup champagne

Place sherbet in a small, chilled dessert dish. Top with crème de cassis and champagne. Serve immediately.

BELLINI

Here is an easy dessert. Use a sweet champagne.

1 scoop peach sherbet
fresh raspberries
⅓ cup champagne

Place sherbet and raspberries in a small, chilled dessert dish. Add champagne and serve immediately.

STRAWBERRIES ROMANOFF SUNDAE

Make this when ripe, juicy strawberries are at their best.

3-4 fresh stemmed sliced strawberries
8-10 fresh raspberries
1 tbs. kirsch, or strawberry-flavored liqueur
1 tbs. *Raspberry Sauce*, page 117
1 scoop vanilla ice cream
whipped cream for garnish

Combine strawberries, raspberries, kirsch and *Raspberry Sauce*. Place ice cream in a chilled serving dish. Pour strawberry mixture over ice cream and top with a little whipped cream. Serve immediately.

GRASSHOPPER

This is a refreshing, minty after-dinner drink.

1 tbs. green crème de menthe
1 tbs. brandy
1 cup vanilla ice cream

Place ingredients in a blender and process on HIGH until smooth and creamy. Pour into a 6- to 8-ounce wine glass and serve.

AMARETTO FREEZE

Serve one of these instead of dessert.

1 tbs. amaretto
1 tbs. brandy
1 cup vanilla ice cream

Place ingredients in a blender and process on HIGH until smooth and creamy. Pour into a 6- to 8-ounce wine glass and serve.

VELVET HAMMER

Servings: 1

This drink is smooth, creamy and delicious.

1 tbs. crème de cacao
1 tbs. brandy

1 cup vanilla or chocolate ice cream
½ tsp. vanilla extract

Place ingredients in a blender and process on HIGH until smooth and creamy. Pour into a 6- to 8-ounce wine glass and serve.

TROPICAL BANANA

Servings: 1

This is a grand finale for a spicy dinner.

½ ripe banana, thinly sliced
2 tsp. lime juice
1 tbs. dark rum

1 tbs. superfine sugar
1 cup orange, vanilla or pineapple ice cream

Place ingredients in a blender and process on HIGH until smooth and creamy. Pour into a 6- to 8-ounce wine glass and serve.

STRAWBERRY SMOOTHIE

Strawberries and ice cream make an easy dessert drink.

¼ cup sliced strawberries, fresh or
  frozen
1 tbs. strawberry syrup

1 cup vanilla or strawberry ice cream
1 tbs. Triple Sec, or orange-flavored
  liqueur

Place ingredients in a blender and process on HIGH until smooth and creamy. Pour into a 6- to 8-ounce wine glass and serve.

PEACH CINNAMON DELIGHT

This is a cold variation of peaches and cream.

¼ cup sliced fresh or frozen peaches
1 cup peach or vanilla ice cream
pinch cinnamon

1 tbs. light rum
1 tbs. Triple Sec, or orange-flavored
  liqueur

Place ingredients in a blender and process on HIGH until smooth and creamy. Pour into a 6- to 8-ounce wine glass and serve.

PINEAPPLE BREEZE

Servings: 1

This drink features tropical flavors blended with ice cream.

¼ cup canned crushed pineapple
1 tbs. pineapple juice

2 tbs. light rum
1 cup pineapple or vanilla ice cream

Place ingredients in a blender and process on HIGH until smooth and creamy. Pour into a 6- to 8-ounce wine glass and serve.

MEXICAN CHOCOLATE

Servings: 1

Cinnamon and chocolate are a classic combination. Serve after a Mexican dinner.

1 tbs. crème de cacao
1 tbs. brandy
1 cup *Mexican Chocolate Ice Cream*, page 28

Place ingredients in a blender and process on HIGH until smooth and creamy. Pour into a 6- to 8-ounce wine glass and serve.

ELEGANT DESSERTS

Homemade ice cream always makes a special dessert, but there are times when a more elegant presentation is desired. Use it to make a colorful molded bombe, layer it with fruit and sauces in tall parfait glasses, or serve it in *Baked Alaska*. Several colors of ice cream can be layered, with or without cake, into impressive towers. Softened ice cream spread over a jelly-roll-sized sponge cake can be rolled up into an ice cream roll and frosted with whipped cream.

IDEAS FOR DESSERTS

- Serve scoops of ice cream in small melon or papaya halves and garnish with fresh raspberries, strawberries or blueberries.

- **EASY CHERRIES JUBILEE:** Open a can of pitted Bing cherries with juice and heat in a small saucepan with 2 tbs. brandy. Spoon cherry sauce over dishes of vanilla ice cream.

- An impressive ice cream platter for a crowd: Scoop out several different flavors of ice cream and sherbet into balls. Place on a chilled platter or serving tray and return to the freezer until party time. Garnish platter with fresh washed lemon tree leaves or fresh mint and scatter fresh berries over tray. Serve with ice cream sauce or topping.

- If serving a dessert buffet, place ice cream balls in a large chilled bowl, place in another larger container filled with ice and drizzle with ice cream sauce, or arrange an assortment of sauces and toppings for guests to make their own.

- Make a dessert pizza using cookie dough for the crust. Bake and cool crust, top with scoops of ice cream, and drizzle a combination of ice cream toppings, nuts and syrups over the ice cream. Cut into wedges to serve. This is popular with the younger crowd.

Desserts involving multiple layers or cake take a little time to put together, so plan to start a day or two before serving the dessert to allow time for freezing each layer before adding the next ingredient. It is important to work as quickly as possible when adding the layers. A quick tip for defrosting ice cream: Place a plastic or microwavable container with 2 cups ice cream in the microwave and DEFROST for 45 seconds to 1 minute. Repeat for a few more seconds, if needed. Cut the slightly softened ice cream into small, thin pieces and spread them in the crust with the back of a spoon or your fingers. If the ice cream really gets soft and melts, the texture becomes icy and grainy. Immediately after adding a layer of ice cream, put the dessert back into the freezer and allow the last layer to freeze somewhat firmly before adding another. Sprinkle praline or spoon preserves between layers to add a little texture and flavor contrast. Liqueurs do not freeze, so partially stir them into the ice cream so the next layer will bond.

Frozen ice cream pies will be easier to cut and serve if you wipe the bottom of the pie plate with a towel or sponge dipped in hot water. Dip your knife into hot water and wipe it dry before cutting the individual pie pieces.

FROZEN LEMON ICE BOX PIE

Servings: 6-8

*Make your own **Graham Cracker Cookie Crust**, page 152, or **Ginger Cookie Crust**, page 151, or buy an already prepared crust from the supermarket. This old-time favorite will stand on its own just spooned into dishes. Chill prepared crust in the freezer before spooning in filling.*

1 can (14 oz.) sweetened condensed milk
1 grated lemon peel
¼ cup fresh lemon juice
1½ cups half-and-half
one 8- or 9-inch cookie crust, chilled

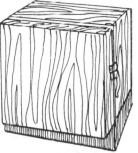

Combine ingredients, except crust, in a blender or food processor and blend until smooth. Cover and chill until ready to freeze. Pour into the ice cream maker and follow the manufacturer's instructions for freezing. Spoon ice cream into chilled pie crust; smooth top. Lightly cover with plastic wrap and place in the freezer. Remove from freezer and put in the refrigerator to soften for about 30 minutes before serving. Cut into wedges and serve.

KEY LIME ICE CREAM PIE

Key lime juice has a very unusual flavor. Some supermarkets carry a bottled Key lime juice, but, if unavailable, substitute ¼ cup each lemon juice and regular lime juice. This is good in **Graham Cracker Cookie Crust***, page 152, or a chocolate cookie crust. The mixture is quite pale, so a little food coloring makes a prettier contrast. Garnish serving plates with thin lime slices.*

1 can (14½ oz.) sweet evaporated milk
⅓ cup Egg Beaters, or egg substitute
½ cup Key lime juice
1 cup half-and-half
few drops green food coloring, optional
one 8- or 9-inch cookie crust, chilled

Combine milk, Egg Beaters, lime juice and half-and-half in a blender or food processor. Blend until well combined. Add food coloring, if desired. Pour into the ice cream maker and follow the manufacturer's instructions for freezing. Spoon ice cream into chilled cookie crust, lightly cover and place in the freezer. Remove from freezer and place in the refrigerator to soften for about 30 minutes before serving. Cut into wedges to serve.

COOKIE CRUSTS

Crushed cookie crumbs make wonderful crusts for ice cream pies. Supermarkets have a variety of ready-to-fill cookie crusts as well as boxes of different flavors of cookie crumbs. The prepared cookie crumbs require just a little sugar and melted butter or margarine to assemble and bake. If you like to make your own, buy or bake cookies, crush them, and either bake or chill them until firm to keep the crumbs from mixing with the ice cream. Baking produces a little more flavorful crust. These can be done ahead, baked and kept in the freezer to be filled on demand. It is important to chill the prepared crust before spooning in the ice cream filling.

GINGER COOKIE CRUST
Makes: one 8-inch shell

*This crust makes a terrific accompaniment for **Spicy Pumpkin**, page 64, **Pumpkin Pecan**, page 65, or **Creamy Peanut Butter Ice Cream**, page 40.*

1 cup (about 5 oz.) finely crushed *Crisp Gingersnaps*, page 128
3 tbs. melted butter
2 tbs. sugar

Combine ingredients, mixing well. Form and bake as directed for *Graham Cracker Cookie Crust*, page 152.

GRAHAM CRACKER COOKIE CRUST

Use a food processor to crush the crumbs, or use a rolling pin and crush the crackers between 2 sheets of waxed paper.

1½ cups finely crushed graham cracker crumbs (about 6 oz.)
¼ cup melted butter
3 tbs. brown sugar
⅛ tsp. cinnamon
1 tbs. Triple Sec, or orange-flavored liqueur

Preheat the oven to 350°. Combine crumbs with butter, sugar and cinnamon, mixing well. Add Triple Sec. Press crumb mixture evenly into a 9-inch pie plate or tart pan. If you have 2 pans the same size, distribute the crumbs as evenly as possible in 1 pan and press the second pan on top of the crumbs to make a dense, smooth crust. Bake for 8 to 10 minutes until crust is firm and lightly browned. Remove to a rack. Cool. Chill in the freezer before filling with ice cream.

GRAHAM CRACKER NUT CRUST

Nuts add to the texture and flavor of a basic graham cracker crust.

¾ cup finely crushed graham cracker crumbs (about 3 oz.)
¼ cup ground toasted walnuts, pecans or almonds
¼ cup melted butter
3 tbs. brown sugar

Combine ingredients, mixing well. Form and bake as directed for *Graham Cracker Cookie Crust*, page 152.

MERINGUE SHELLS

Makes: two 9-inch layers

Meringue shells are very versatile and can be used for texture contrast separating layers of ice cream or whipped cream, or they can be filled with ice cream to create an ice cream pie. Individual meringue shells (about 3 inches in diameter) make elegant serving bowls for ice cream and sauce.

4 egg whites
pinch salt
1⅓ cups sugar

1 tsp. vanilla extract
1 tsp. lemon juice

Preheat the oven to 275°. Line baking sheets with parchment paper or foil. Trace two 9-inch circles on parchment paper or foil. Beat egg whites and salt in a mixer until soft peaks form. Gradually whip in sugar, vanilla and lemon juice. Egg whites should look very smooth and glossy. Using a pastry tube with a large tip, or a spoon and spatula, fill circles with an even layer of meringue. Bake for about 1 hour, until crisp and dry. Remove from oven and allow to cool to room temperature. If the air is quite humid, turn off the oven and allow meringues to remain in oven until completely cool.

To make individual shells, trace ten to twelve 2½- to 3-inch circles and spread meringue mixture inside circles. Bake until crisp and dry, about 1 hour. Store in an airtight container and fill with ice cream and sauce just before serving.

ICE CREAM COOKIE SANDWICHES AND BARS

Your favorite cookies, large or small, can be filled with a flavorful ice cream and placed in the freezer for a quick dessert treat for children and adults. Soften the ice cream. Either put it in a pastry bag fitted with a large tip and pipe it onto the flat side of 1 cookie, or carefully spoon the ice cream over 1 cookie, topping with another cookie. Place in the freezer until firm and then wrap each sandwich in plastic wrap for easy storing.

Consider filling *Crisp Gingersnaps*, page 128, with *Spicy Pumpkin Ice Cream*, page 64, or *Creamy Peanut Butter Ice Cream*, page 40. Sandwich chocolate cookies with *Easy Caramel Ice Cream*, page 19, *Mexican Chocolate Ice Cream*, page 28, or *Cognac Ice Cream*, page 26.

Mix and bake cookie dough in an 8-inch square baking pan. Cut into squares and top each square with a scoop of ice cream and a flavor-compatible sauce. Or spread softened ice cream over the baked, cooled cookie dough, cover and freeze. Cut into squares to serve and top with whipped cream, chocolate sprinkles, toasted coconut or a luscious sauce.

CASSATA

This Italian-style dessert starts with a prepared pound cake. Serve in thin slices.

prepared pound cake
softened ice cream, sherbet or combination
brandy, or fruit-flavored liqueur
whipped cream, optional
strawberry, apricot or chocolate sauce, optional

Cut cake horizontally into 3 or 4 layers. Spread each layer with softened ice cream, sherbet or a combination. Sprinkle each layer with a few drops of brandy. Assemble cake. Frost with whipped cream, or serve without whipped cream frosting and pass a fresh strawberry, apricot or chocolate sauce.

ICE CREAM-FILLED ANGEL FOOD CAKE

Ice cream-filled cakes are birthday party and shower favorites. They also make a special Easter or Sunday dinner dessert. Sprinkle the inside of the cake with a little liqueur or orange juice before spooning in the ice cream. Frost the cake with the whipped cream topping just before serving. The cake may be garnished with fresh sliced strawberries or peaches, raspberries, chopped nuts or grated chocolate, or it may be drizzled with an ice cream syrup to complement the ice cream filling.

1 prebaked tube angel food cake, 10-inch diameter (10 oz.)
1 tbs. liqueur, or orange juice, optional
2-3 cups ice cream or sherbet, slightly softened
1 cup heavy cream
1 tbs. sugar
1 tbs. vanilla extract
finely chopped nuts, grated chocolate, toasted flaked coconut,
   ice cream syrup or fresh fruit for garnish

Prepare cake by cutting a ¾-inch slice from top of cake. Make a tunnel in the cake using a long, thin-bladed knife. Cut in about ¾ inch from outside of cake and from center of cake. Cut down about 1 to 2 inches, leaving about a 1-inch bottom layer.

Carefully pull out cake from shell and reserve for another use. Sprinkle cake shell with liqueur, if desired, and spoon in softened ice cream. Replace top slice, cover cake and place in the freezer. Remove cake to the refrigerator about 30 minutes before serving. Whip heavy cream with sugar and vanilla until stiff peaks form. Frost top and sides of cake. Sprinkle with nuts, grated chocolate, toasted flaked coconut or ice cream syrup, or top with fresh fruit slices.

SOME DELICIOUS COMBINATIONS

- *Rich Strawberry Ice Cream*, page 32, with fresh sliced strawberries for top of cake
- *Easy Caramel Ice Cream*, page 19, layered with a little chocolate sauce, with chopped pecans on top of cake
- vanilla ice cream layered with a little *Raspberry Sauce*, page 117
- *Mexican Chocolate Ice Cream*, page 28, with chocolate syrup whipped into heavy cream, topped with toasted chopped almonds

ICE CREAM CAKE ROLL

Ice cream cake rolls make a pretty presentation and can be done ahead of time. Bake the cake a few hours or even a day ahead so there is time to cool and chill it before filling with softened ice cream. **Old-Fashioned Lemon Ice Cream**, *page 34, makes a terrific filling. Combine your favorite flavors to create a sensational dessert.*

CAKE

4 eggs
1 tsp. baking powder
½ tsp. salt
¾ cup sugar

1 tsp. vanilla extract
¾ cup sifted cake flour
powdered sugar

---

3 cups softened ice cream
1 cup heavy cream, whipped
¼ cup superfine or powdered sugar

chopped nuts, grated chocolate,
    flaked coconut or instant cocoa
    mix for garnish

Preheat the oven to 375°. Oil a 10-x-15-inch jelly roll pan and line it with parchment or waxed paper. Oil paper liner and lightly dust with flour. Combine eggs, baking powder and salt in a mixer bowl and beat until eggs are thick and lemon-colored. Gradually beat in sugar. Add vanilla and fold in flour. Spread batter evenly in prepared pan and bake for 10 to 12 minutes, until lightly browned. Spread a kitchen towel on the counter; sift a light layer of powdered sugar over towel. Remove cake from oven and turn out on towel. Remove paper liner. Cut off crisp cake edges and gently roll up cake starting with short side, with towel inside the roll. Cool and chill cake in the refrigerator. When ready to fill cake roll, gently unroll cake, remove towel and spread with ice cream to within ½ inch of edges. Re-roll cake and place in the freezer. Whip cream with 3 tbs. sugar until soft peaks form. Spread over cake roll and sprinkle with desired garnish. As soon as whipped cream has firmed, cover cake with plastic wrap and foil, and freeze for several hours before serving. Place cake in refrigerator about 30 minutes before serving. Cut into slices to serve.

VARIATIONS

- Sprinkle ice cream layer with 1 cup finely chopped, toasted nuts.
- Lightly drizzle a few tablespoons strawberry or chocolate ice cream syrup over inside of cake before spreading with ice cream.
- Spread thin layer of strawberry, apricot or blackberry preserves over inside of cake before spreading with ice cream.

EASY SPONGE CAKE

*This is a quick cake with many variations. Serve it with a scoop of almost any flavor ice cream. Layer it with **Mexican Chocolate Ice Cream**, page 28, and **Rich Vanilla Custard Ice Cream**, page 46, to make a luscious ice cream cake. Use lemon extract and grated lemon peel, or almond extract in addition to the vanilla to accent other ice cream flavors.*

2 eggs
⅓ cup sugar
1 tsp. vanilla extract
⅓ cup flour
½ tsp. baking powder
pinch salt

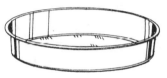

Preheat the oven to 375°. Butter an 8-inch round cake pan and line bottom of pan with parchment or waxed paper. Beat eggs with a mixer until fluffy and lemon-colored. Gradually beat in sugar and add vanilla. Sift together flour, baking powder and salt; fold into cake mixture. Pour into prepared baking pan and bake for about 12 to 14 minutes until cake springs back lightly when touched. Remove from oven and place on a cooling rack. Allow cake to cool. Makes 1 layer, about 1 inch thick.

For individual ice cream cakes, split cake layer in half horizontally with a long, sharp knife. Choose deep-sided soufflé cups or molds and cut cake into rounds a little smaller than the cup diameter. Spray cups with nonstick cooking spray. Make 2 strips of foil or plastic wrap about 8 inches long for each cup and place in cups with tabs extending over the sides of the cup. Place 1 piece of cake in the bottom of each mold, spread cake with a thin layer of softened ice cream and top with another piece of cake. Place cups in freezer for 1 hour before continuing with another flavor of ice cream and more cake. When molds are full, cover with plastic wrap and freeze until ready to use. These can be kept in the freezer for 3 or 4 days, tightly wrapped. To serve, remove from freezer and carefully cut around edge of mold to release cake. Pull cake out of cup using foil or plastic wrap tags. Place on individual serving dishes and refrigerate for about 30 minutes to soften before serving.

To soften frozen ice cream, microwave 1 pint, lightly covered, on DEFROST for 45 seconds to 1 minute. Stir ice cream with a spoon to make the right spreading consistency.

FLAMING STRAWBERRIES

When making this very elegant dessert, have the ice cream ready in chilled dessert bowls because it only takes a couple of minutes to heat the strawberries. Expand the recipe for the desired number of servings.

¼ cup orange juice
2 tbs. sugar
1 cup sliced strawberries
3 tbs. brandy
2 scoops vanilla ice cream

Place orange juice and sugar in a small heavy saucepan and stir over medium heat until sugar dissolves and orange juice has thickened slightly. Add strawberries and heat through. Pour in brandy; allow to heat for a few seconds. Using a fireplace match, carefully flame brandy. Be very careful to avert your face. This should be done under a stove hood or an area where flames will not be in contact with anything flammable. Immediately pour over ice cream in chilled bowls and serve.

PARFAITS

Parfaits are made of layers of ice cream and toppings. They can be done ahead, covered and kept in the freezer until ready to serve. Use tall parfait glasses or improvise with heavy duty large wine glasses and chill them in the refrigerator or freezer before filling. Part of the charm of this dessert is seeing the contrasting layers. One quart of ice cream will make 4 to 6 servings, depending on the size of the parfait glasses.

PARFAIT IDEAS

- Layer *Apple Cinnamon Sherbet*, page 82, with caramel syrup and ginger cookie or gingerbread crumbs. Garnish with a little whipped cream.

- Layer *Frozen Zabaglione Ice Cream*, page 35, with *Zinfandel Sauce*, page 120, and toasted sliced almonds.

- Layer *Old-Fashioned Lemon Ice Cream*, page 34, or *Lemon Cheesecake Ice Cream*, page 55, with *Blueberry Sauce*, page 119, and a few fresh blueberries.

- Layer *Mexican Chocolate Ice Cream*, page 28, with chocolate syrup and chocolate cookie crumbs. Top with a little whipped cream.

MOLDED ICE CREAM BOMBES

Contrasting layers of ice cream or sherbet are packed into an ice cream mold or bowl, frozen, unmolded and sliced into serving portions. The ice cream or sherbet must be softened enough to spread with the back of a spoon. Microwave on DEFROST for 45 to 60 seconds, repeating as necessary for the amount of ice cream you are softening, or place ice cream in the refrigerator for 30 minutes before using. It takes time to create a bombe because each layer must be frozen before the next is added. It may be more practical to buy some of the ice cream flavors to save time.

A 6-cup mold will make about 8 servings; an 8-cup mold will make about 8 to 10 servings. Chill the mold in the freezer for about 30 minutes before starting.

There are no set rules regarding number of layers or flavor combinations, so use your imagination. One of the layers can be heavy cream whipped with a liqueur, or fruit and nuts can be added to softened vanilla ice cream to create a special flavor. Fresh fruit can be sweetened and folded into whipped cream to make a refreshing contrasting layer.

Once you have made an ice cream bombe, you will see that the process is quite simple if you allow yourself enough time to do it in easy steps.

RAINBOW BOMBE

*This is a 4-layer delight. Serve it with **Zinfandel Sauce**, page 120.*

1 qt. *Holiday Eggnog Ice Cream*,
   page 43, or vanilla ice cream
   mixed with a little dark rum and
   maraschino cherries

1 pt. *Pistachio Nut Ice Cream*, page 37
1 pt. raspberry sherbet
½ cup heavy cream
¼ cup instant cocoa mix

Chill an 8-cup mold in the freezer. Soften eggnog ice cream. Evenly layer the inside of mold with a 1½-inch layer of ice cream, leaving a deep well in the center. Place mold in the freezer to harden completely, about an hour. When ready to continue, soften pistachio ice cream. Make another layer inside the mold about ¾-inch thick, leaving a well in the center. Return mold to freezer for another hour. Soften raspberry sherbet. Line mold with a thin, even layer of sherbet. Return mold to freezer for an hour. Whip cream with cocoa until stiff peaks form. Completely fill center of mold with whipped cream. Cover mold and place in freezer. When ready to serve, quickly dip mold into a bowl filled with hot water for a few seconds; then invert mold over a chilled serving plate. If necessary, apply a hot kitchen towel to mold to get it to release. Cut into wedges with a sharp, hot knife to serve. Pour a thin layer of sauce around each piece and serve immediately.

INDEX

SERVE CREATIVE, EASY, NUTRITIOUS MEALS WITH Nitty Gritty® COOKBOOKS

Sautés
Cooking in Porcelain
Appetizers
Recipes for the Loaf Pan
Casseroles
The Best Bagels are made at home*
   (*perfect for your bread machine)
The Toaster Oven Cookbook
Skewer Cooking on the Grill
Creative Mexican Cooking
Extra-Special Crockery Pot Recipes
Cooking in Clay
Marinades
Deep Fried Indulgences
Cooking with Parchment Paper
The Garlic Cookbook
Flatbreads From Around the World
From Your Ice Cream Maker
Favorite Cookie Recipes
Cappuccino/Espresso: The Book of
   Beverages
Indoor Grilling

Slow Cooking
The Best Pizza is made at home*
   (*perfect for your bread machine)
The Well Dressed Potato
Convection Oven Cookery
The Steamer Cookbook
The Pasta Machine Cookbook
The Versatile Rice Cooker
The Dehydrator Cookbook
The Bread Machine Cookbook
The Bread Machine Cookbook II
The Bread Machine Cookbook III
The Bread Machine Cookbook IV:
   Whole Grains and Natural Sugars
The Bread Machine Cookbook V:
   Favorite Recipes from 100 Kitchens
The Bread Machine Cookbook VI:
   *Hand-Shaped Breads from the
   Dough Cycle*
Worldwide Sourdoughs From Your
   Bread Machine
Recipes for the Pressure Cooker

The New Blender Book
The Sandwich Maker Cookbook
Waffles
The Coffee Book
The Juicer Book
The Juicer Book II
Bread Baking (traditional)
No Salt, No Sugar, No Fat Cookbook
Cooking for 1 or 2
Quick and Easy Pasta Recipes
The 9x13 Pan Cookbook
Extra-Special Crockery Pot Recipes
Low Fat American Favorites
Now That's Italian!
Fabulous Fiber Cookery
Low Salt, Low Sugar, Low Fat Desserts
Healthy Cooking on the Run
Muffins, Nut Breads and More
The Wok
New Ways to Enjoy Chicken
Favorite Seafood Recipes
New International Fondue Cookbook

For a free catalog, write or call:
Bristol Publishing Enterprises, Inc.
P.O. Box 1737
San Leandro, CA 94577
(800) 346-4889; in California, (510) 895-4461